For the Poor and For the Gentry:

Mary Healy remembers
her life

Mary Healy

Geography **P**ublications

In memory of my husband.

Published in Ireland by
Geography Publications
24, Kennington Road,
Templeogue, Dublin 6W

ISBN: 0 906602 15 7

Cover design by Margaret Lonergan, Carrick-on-Suir

Design & Typesetting by Typeform Ltd, Clonshaugh, Dublin 17.

Printed by Genprint, Clonshaugh, Dublin 17.

Contents

Acknowledgements

I wish to thank the following for their help: Mr and Mrs Pierce O'Donnell, Grangebeg, Mrs Ponsonby, Miss Agnes Allen, Mr Austin O'Flynn, Mrs Caroline Palmer, Mr and Mrs Sean Hanrahan, Miss Mary McCarthy, Mrs Hazleton, Mrs Goodbody, Mr Joe Kenny, The Fethard Historical Society and particularly my grand-daughter, Mary Hurley, who typed the first part of my book. I am also indebted to my daughter-in-law, Phyllis, who typed the second part and helped me with the proof reading.

Fethard

Where the grey Clashawley glides,
And the bashful brickeen hides,
There my heart for aye abides
My native Fethard.

Those grand old walls that silent stand
To mark an era in our land,
Crumbling not to Cromwell's hand
Staunch walls of Fethard.

Nestled in the cosy hills,
Fed by crystal sparkling rills,
Whetting wheels of busy mills
My native Fethard.

Heather headed Slievenamon
Snatches first sweet streaks of dawn,
And smiling, mirrors all upon
Old misty Fethard.

The weird wild woods of grand old Grove
The haunts that Gods and angels love
Tow'r sentinels serene above
To guard old Fethard.

Like a velvet verdant vein
Stretches old Kiltinan's plain
Maze of wood and leafy lane
Around old Fethard.

The furze-clad hills at even-time,
Echo sweet soft notes sublime
Not grander chime in any clime
Than bells of Fethard.

I'm longing to be back among
Those grand old scenes when Nature's tongue,
Tells every heart that life is young,
In ancient Fethard.

    T.J. KEATING, Brookhill, Fethard.

Chapter 1

Childhood in Kilkenny

I was born in the city of Kilkenny on the 12th September 1912. I always answer if I am asked what year I was born, 1912, and add, a momentous year, for the Ulster Volunteers were formed, the Labour Party was formed in Clonmel, and the 'unsinkable' Titanic went down. In the house where I was born and reared, I cannot remember ever being cool in the summer or warm in the winter. The heat was hard to bear, but the cold was worse, cold which only for we being young and hopeful, would have taken all the joy out of our lives. Our house was high above the river Nore, with no houses in front, but with an elbow high wall at the other side of the road. Inside this wall and leading down to the quay was a field which belonged to Saint John's Parish, to which parish we belonged. The parish school was in this field and to this school in due course, I and my four brothers went. One part of the school was for infants, up to first class and the other part up to sixth class. We never said first standard or second standard, but always class. The two Miss Reids and Mrs. Andrews taught in the infants school. The Miss Reids were sisters and were always called little Miss Reid and big Miss Reid, for one of them was small and plump and the other, was what one would call a fine figure of a woman, tall and broad. We all started school at three years of age and when we finished in the infant's school, the boys went to the Monastery school on the Dublin road and the girls to the senior school next door. Little Miss Reid, who was the principal of the infants school, always kissed the boys who were leaving, but never the girls. We thought this very unfair, we would have considered it a great honour to be kissed by the teacher.

Mrs. Gibbs was the principal in the senior school, she had an assistant named Miss Dwyer. Mrs. Gibbs was a big motherly looking woman who had several children of her own. I have no fond memories of either of them and for all of Mrs. Gibbs motherly looks, to me she appeared a cold forbidding woman. Miss Dwyer I find difficult to describe, she hasn't stayed in my mind like the other teachers. I know that between ourselves we called her cock-nosed Dwyer, as she had a small turned up nose. My mother used to tell me that Miss Dwyer had 'notions' of my father before he married my mother, be that as it may, she never married. The mothers of the children who lived in our street used to bring down the lunch at one o'clock, and hand it over the wall of the playground to the children. One day when my mother brought down the lunch, she said to little Miss Reid, 'I'm going to "breech" Jack this week'. 'Don't, said Miss Reid, 'I won't be half as fond of him then'. He was then four years old and was still in petticoats and a skirt.

My father Jim Loughman, was a tailor, employed in the asylum. The word asylum did not mean to us children, a refuge, a sanctuary, as defined in the dictionary, but a place where mad people were locked up. My father was a great reader, and from what the neighbours used to say, a very intelligent man. My brother Paddy was the eldest of the family, then Jack, then Jim, whom we used to call Bimmy, on account of my father being Jim. I was next, the only girl. After me came Billy, the last of the family. Bimmy was, what we used to call in those days, simple, now we say mentally retarded. My mother always blamed the midwife who attended her at his birth. She used to say that all the time she was in labour she never stopped examining her internally. He was very docile and lovable. On a moonlight night, he'd go out the back, stand at the wall of the coalhouse and sing William Kenealy's beautiful song, 'The Moon Behind the Hill'. He had a beautiful singing voice. Everybody loved him and felt protective towards him. The man who was gardener with the Church of Ireland Bishop, used to pass up our street morning and evening on his way to work, (he lived in Maudlin Street). He always stopped to talk to Bimmy. When the first apples were ripe he would bring him some from the Palace gardens. He always used to say to my mother, 'Isn't it a grand thing to be the mother of a saint'.

Bimmy also was an epileptic, and would fall down in an epileptic fit without any warning. My mother used to say that wherever Jack was, he always seemed to be near to help her when Bimmy had a fit. I think Jack was her favourite among us children, although she would be very indignant and deny it if we said such a thing. From Michael Street where we lived we had the most beautiful view in the city. We could see the castle, Saint Canice's Cathedral, Saint Mary's Cathedral, The Tholsel, which we usually called the Town Hall and the ruins of Saint Francis Abbey, after which Smithwick's brewery was named has always been vivid in my memory because during the Civil War, one morning a Free State soldier came in through our back door and without a word to anyone went upstairs. I sat as far away from the kitchen window as possible, in case a shot would come through it, but my mother wasn't afraid, and she followed him upstairs and asked him what he intended doing. 'There's a fellow over behind a barrel in the brewery yard and I'm trying to get a shot at him' he replied. The 'fellow' being a Republican soldier. He didn't shoot at him however, but went away again. That same night a number of Free State soldiers took over the upstairs bedrooms of the Geoghegan family who lived eight doors up from us, barricaded the windows with the mattresses off the beds and again went away without firing a shot.

The house where I was born was owned by Kilkenny Corporation, and was described on the rent receipt as an artisan's dwelling. The lowest rent we paid, in my memory, was three and sixpence weekly. I suppose according to the standards of those days they were good sized houses, but badly planned. There was a narrow hall with the back door facing the front door, and almost always the front door was left open, with the result, that, if it was a windy day, when anyone opened the back door, my mother would exclaim, 'Jesus Mary and Joseph save us'. She was always terrified any of us would get hurt if the door banged on us. There was a sitting room and a kitchen to the left of the hall and the stairs to the right, which led to three bedrooms. There was a yard at the back of the house, in which was built a dry lavatory, and coal house. Outside the yard a passage-way ran at the back of the house, up which anyone in our row could bring a load of coal or manure for the garden. At the end of the garden there was a sandpit, from which the Corporation drew sand. Leading down to the sandpit from our garden was an incline and down this incline the contents of the bucket from the lavatory was thrown.

My brother Paddy always helped my mother to carry the bucket. One night he said to her , 'Mammy, wait until you hear the plop' — she thought this was very funny. This excrement was never covered, so it wasn't any wonder that infectious diseases were rampant, noticeably diphtheria and scarlet fever. There was a pump where we got water at the end of our row of houses. We children always carried the water when we were big enough. Where I live now, the pump, or fountain, as some people called it, was always called 'The Judy'. Nobody seems to know why this name, but I often wonder if it is because women supply sustenance during the early part of a child's life, and the water, which we cannot survive without, got a female name at its source. We had an open fire in the kitchen, raised off the floor, with a hob at each side, and on this fire all meals were cooked; water was boiled for to make tea, and of course to wash the clothes in a zinc bath. We children hated to see the bath on the floor when we came home from school. The kitchen was narrow and dark, and to this day it has been associated in my mind with squalor and misery.

When I was two years old my father developed a cough. My mother

3

was worried about this, as several of his brothers and sisters had died from tuberculosis. After some persuasion he agreed to go to the doctor attached to the mental hospital, a doctor Buggy. He examined my father and after the examination said to him, I think you had better see Doctor Heffernan. When my father came home and told my mother, she knew it was tantamount to a sentence of death, for Dr. Heffernan was the T.B. doctor. In those days there was no cure for T.B. My father had to come out on pension then, a pension which was very small, as he hadn't long enough service to qualify for a full pension. We were very poor, in worldly goods at any rate, but rich in our family life and our neighbours. Looking back now at my childhood, the worst part of it was the cold, the icy cold bed at night, especially in the winter when it would often be many hours before I could fall asleep. The morning would be as bad, stepping out on to bare floor boards, then down the stairs to a cold cement floored kitchen, an open fire between two high hobs, the heat going mostly up the chimney. Hell to me has always appeared as intensely cold, instead of intensely hot. I suppose, too, we lived in the coldest part of the city, for my mother used to say it was like 'Spion Kop', which I discovered afterwards was a place in South Africa, which, to the best of my knowledge must have been mentioned during the Boer War. My mother also told us, that until, and during the Boer War, British soldiers wore red uniforms and were an easy target for the Boers, the colour of whose uniforms they afterwards copied.

My father lived for four years after he came out on pension. He was able to live a fairly normal life for a couple of years and spent a few months in Peamount sanatorium. He hated being there and always complained that the patients got margarine instead of butter. This seemed to be the biggest complaint he had, but I don't think he was very happy there. My mother brought me to see him one day, but I don't remember seeing him at all, but I do remember being brought into the D.B.C. and getting tea and buns. It's the longest memory I have. We were, like almost all working class Irish people, Roman Catholics. My mother worried terribly about the fact that my father was not what one would call an orthodox Catholic. He didn't believe in Transubstantiation. Time and again the priests of our parish would come to visit him, but they would not give him Holy Communion. My mother worried terribly over this. She thought he would never go to heaven if he didn't believe what the Church taught. In the last months of my father's life she often sat up with him all night. She used to worry about his soul and he not conforming to all the teachings of the Church. She also told us children, of how cold she used to be on the nights she had to sit up with him, when he used to be gasping for breath. He died in the month of January 1919. Most of the nights of

4

that winter she was up at night with him. He had to have the window open at the top and the bottom and my mother used to have to wear a coat and a scarf to try and keep warm. They were terrible times for the poor, for nobody ever had heat, except for a fire in the kitchen, and often that was only a small one.

In Saint John's Parish, to which we belonged, there were three priests, an administrator and two curates. I cannot remember the name of the administrator, but the curates names were, Fr. Gibbons and Fr. Mackey. Fr. Gibbons held very orthodox views, but Fr. Mackey was fairly liberal, for those days at any rate. When my father was near death my mother somehow got around him to let her send for a priest and she sent Paddy over immediately to the presbytery to ask one of the priests to come over. Shen then went back upstairs to my father, and he said to her, 'I hope they don't send Fr. Gibbons', so she went downstairs and sent Jack hot foot after Paddy to ask for Fr. Mackey. He did hear my father's confession, and gave him Holy Communion, and the way he got around my father's unbelief in transubstantiation was, by saying to him, 'will you receive Holy Communion, even though you do not believe in transubstantiation, but because the church teaches it!' My father acquiesced, and my mother was happy, for although she was an intelligent woman she believed that if my father died without complying with the rules of the church he would never go to heaven. I don't know if she thought he would be damned, and I don't know where she thought he would go, but she thought he would not go to heaven. Fr. Gibbons, in many discussions with my father, used to tell him that he read too much for his own good. Why this should be I do not know, unless it was that well read people might be more of a threat to the established order of things. When my father died I was six years old, the eldest of our family, Paddy, was eleven.

Shortly after this time my father's brother, Dick Loughman, who was foreman printer with the *Kilkenny Journal* called to our home and told my mother that there was a vacancy in Statham's garage for an apprentice as a motor car body builder, and Paddy could get the job if my mother was willing. Paddy started work at eleven years of age and that was the end of his childhood. Looking back now, it was terribly sad that he did not get a chance of a good education. He would not have got very far at school anyway, for a great many of the teachers were sadists, and believed that beating children would make them learn. One day Paddy came home from school with lacerated thighs, caused by been beaten with a cane. I will never forget the tears of my mother, tears of helplessness and hopelessness, for it was an accepted thing that there was no redress. The child must have deserved it, it was always said, but Paddy was a quiet retiring child and it was for not knowing one of his lessons that he was beaten. My mother kept him at home, and away from school for, to the best of my memory, one week. At the end of the week Brother Peter, the Brother who had beaten Paddy, called to our house to ask why Paddy hadn't been at school. My mother told him, and to the best of my knowledge he wasn't beaten after that.

We children loved Christmas. It was not for the toys we got for more often than not, we would not get one toy at all, but, like Mr. Micawber, we lived in the hope that 'something would turn up'. The most we would get in our stocking would be an apple and an orange. Before Christmas my mother would make one big plum pudding. She would boil it in a cloth, in a big iron pot over the open fire. It would take about six hours to cook, she would then take it up and hang it from a nail in the wall until Christmas day, when she would boil it again for two hours. We would have a chicken and a piece of bacon, potatoes, always celery and white sauce and jelly for the sweet course as well as the pudding. Bimmy had a ditty which he always sung during the first boiling of the pudding, the following are some of the words:

> O, Thy very nicest,
> Round and round and hot
> See the big plum pudding,
> Bubbling in the pot.

The lovely highlight and neighbourliness of Christmas, to me at any rate, was midnight. Everyone would be out on the street wishing each other a Happy Christmas and the bells of St. Canice's Cathedral would peal out in honour of the birth of our Saviour. There was no Midnight Mass when I was a child, but six o'clock morning Mass was the one to which the woman of the house went, so that she would have plenty of time to prepare the dinner. We would always have our breakfast around eight o'clock, and when it was over, my mother would go to O'Keeffe's next door, where Mrs. O'Keeffe and herself would have a half glass of whiskey. Apart from that, we never went outside the door again on Christmas Day.

Saint Stephen's Day was a great day for us children, for the Wren Boys came around. My brothers, and a great many of the boys of our street, went as Wren Boys, but they always called themselves Mummers. Some of the parents wouldn't allow their sons to go, those parents whom my mother described as thinking themselves 'a step above buttermilk!' The boys would all have their faces blackened, and some of them would be dressed as women, mostly long black skirts and blouses belonging to their mothers, and the rest of them in their father's old clothes. They always had a musical instrument, usually a melodion. They entered the house saying:

> Here we come the Mummer Boys,
> We come here to make no noise,
> We come here to sport and play,
> Always on the Mummers' Day,
> And if you don't believe in what I say enter in,

And here my memory fails me. I know there was a character intended to be the devil, and the words he was introduced with were:

> Here I come Beelzebub,
> Under my arm I carry my drum,
> In my hand a frying pan and I call myself
> A jolly old man,
> And if you don't believe in what I say enter in the old soldier
> The old soldier stepped forward and said,
> 'Here I come the old soldier from the war I have sprung;
> without a stitch on my back,
> or a stitch on my bum.
> Here I come Saint Patrick the patron of the land
> I banish snakes and serpents with my holy wand
> I bless the land of Erin, I bless it o'er and o'er,
>   and in memory of Saint Patrick the shamrock
>   will be worn.
> And if you don't believe in what I say enter in.'

He says more but the tableau finishes with the doctor being called, after one of those taking part is supposed to have collapsed. The head of the group called out, 'A doctor, a doctor', and when the doctor steps forward says to him, 'what can you cure doctor'. The doctor answers: 'I can cure the plague within, and the plague without, bring up an old woman ten score and ten, with the knuckle bone of her big toe out and I'll put it in again, I have a little bottle here in my waistcoat pocket called inky pinky jolly go dinky, and three drops of this will cure him.' The doctor puts a small bottle to the lips of the collapsed one, and he recovers completely.

The group then filed out of the house singing in unison the following words:

> The wran the wran the king of all birds
> Saint Stephen's Day he was caught in the furze.
> Although he was little his family was great.
> So help us great lady to lay him in state.

7

We hunted him up, and we hunted him down,
We hunted him in to Bagnelstown,
We fired a shot and broke his pate,
And buried him under the avenue gate,
Up with the kettle and down with the pan,
Give us our money and we'll all be gone.

They always got a few pence in each house, no matter how poor the people were, and most of us were poor in those days. There was a doggeral, which we children used to recite every now and again, and it went as follows:

'If ever you go to Kilkenny,
Look out for the hole in the wall.
Its there you'll get eggs for a penny
    and 'butther' for nothing at all.
And when you get under the blankets,
The bugs will all sheil you with stones.'

I cannot remember if there was more to it, but I know there is a version of it now which is recited for tourists, and which brings in Kilkenny cats, but I don't think cats were ever mentioned in it when I was a child. There is no word 'sheil' in the Dictionary, but it meant pelt to us.

The biggest disappointments I got when I was a child, was over a celluloid doll which was in the window of Tallis's shop in Rose Inn street. I was very shy and retiring and one day on our way home from school I asked Kitty O'Brien, who was a school friend of mine, would she go into Tallis's shop and ask how much was the doll. She was told the doll was two pence. I thought Saturday would never come, when I would have two pence to buy the doll. But when I went into Tallis's on Saturday, I found they had made a mistake, and the doll was tenpence. It might as well have been ten pounds, for no way could I get tenpence. I find it hard to believe now, that money was so scarce, but scarce it was, for my mother was ever only able to afford to put one penny into the collection box at the Church door at Sunday Mass, and sometimes only a halfpenny, and this was usual for working class people. But if we were poor in material things, we were rich in the culture of our home life, for my mother used to tell us stories and read poetry to us. The poems which have always stayed in my mind are, 'We Are Seven' by, I think, Wordsworth. 'Caoch the Piper', and 'The Dark Girl At The Holy Well', both written by John Keegan. They were in one of four books belonging to my father, entitled *The Cabinet of Irish Literature*. She also read for us Goldsmith's *Deserted Village*. We loved 'Caoch the Piper', it appealed most to our sentiments, although now I know that the dog in the poem, named 'Pinch', could not have been alive when Caoch returned to the once happy home twenty years later. To me now, 'The Dark Girl At The Holy Well' is the most beautiful. I have the book which contains the poem before me now as I write, and I think the beauty of the poem may be seen in the following verses:

THE DARK GIRL AT THE HOLY WELL
Mother is that the passing bell?
Or yet the midnight chime?
Or rush of angels golden wings?
Or is it near the time —
The time when God they say comes down.
This weary world upon,
With holy Mary at his right,
And at his left Saint John?

'I'm Dumb' my heart forgets to throb,
My blood forgets to run;
But vain my sighs — in vain I sob —
God's will must still be done.
I hear but tone of warning bell
For holy priest or nun;
On earth God's face I'll never see;
Nor Mary, nor Saint John.

"Mother my hopes are gone again –
My heart is black as ever"
Mother I say look forth once more.
And see can you discover
Gods glory in the crimson clouds –
See does he ride upon
That perfumed breeze – or do you see
The Virgin or Saint John.

Ah no, Ah no, Well God Of Peace
Grant me thy blessing still
Oh, make me patient with my doom,
And happy at thy will,
And guide my footsteps so on earth,
That, when I'm dead and gone,
My eyes may catch thy shining light,
With Mary and Saint John.

Yet mother, could I see thy smile,
before we part below,
Or watch the silver moon and stars,
Where Slaney's ripples flow,
Oh! could I see the sweet sun shine,
My native hills upon,
I'd never love my God the less,
Nor Mary, nor Saint John.

But no, ah no, it cannot be,
Yet, mother, do not mourn;\
Come kneel again, and pray to God,
In peace let us return.
The dark girls doom must aye be mine,
But heaven will light me on,
Until I find my way to God,
And Mary and Saint John.

The poet says in a footnote which is as follows: Dark is here used in the sense of blind — It is believed that the waters of Saint John's Well near Kilkenny, possess healing powers and that, as the angel troubled the pool at Bethesda at certain seasons, so, Saint John, the Virgin, and Jesus, would at certain times and at the hour of midnight, descend in the form of three angels in white and pass with lightning speed into the fountain. The patients who saw this wonderful sight were cured; those who only heard the rushing of the wings might still continue to endure their infirmity. In the days of my childhood there was always a bonfire on the hills above Johnswell on the eve of the feast of Saint John. We could see the fire from Michael Street, where we lived. I had never been in Johnswell, nor any farther outside the city than we could walk. None of my friends had bicycles — they were a luxury. We walked as far as Leyrath on the Dublin Road. We always turned back before we reached the gate, as Leyrath House had the name of being haunted, and we were afraid to go even inside the gate, as we all firmly believed in ghosts. We would walk also as far as Dunmore, but were never inside the caves. One of our favourite walks was The Lacken, and sometimes the Canal. We never said the Canal Walk, but always The Canal.

Another of our Sunday pastimes was pooling our halfpennies, and buying a packet of Woodbines and going up to the railway station, getting into a railway carriage and dividing the cigarettes. There were five cigarettes in the packet, and usually four of us children, Kitty Quinn, May Cummins, Kathleen Geoghegan and myself. I can't remember what we did with the extra cigarette, but I know we felt very daring. Those three were the friends of my childhood; although our neighbours to whom we were closest were the Keeffe's, who lived at one side of us, and we seemed to have most in common with them. At the other side of us lived the Butlers, Mrs. Butler and her husband Pat, and their lodger John Lawlor. Pat was a carpenter in the asylum and John was a shoemaker there as well. They were not city born like my father, but had come in from outside the city. John was bestman for my father at his wedding, so they must have been close friends at one time, but Molly Butler (we never called her Mrs.) was so possessive where he was concerned that she appeared to own him. He was a big childlike man, and never seemed to mind. The three of them were fond of the drop, too fond for their own good, for they got blind drunk every pay day. My mother used to say that it was the Butler's who got John Lawlor in on the drink. When all their wages were spent they pawned their best suits until next pay day, which was every month. Finally, tragedy struck. Molly had been in and out of her own house one pay day, abusing all and sundry. She was drunk at the time, and she was very proud that John Lawlor was a member of the Volunteers. Mrs. Keeffe and Mrs. Dowling were in our house the last time she came in. Mrs. Dowling was another neighbour, but we were never close to her like we were to the Keeffe's. Molly started bragging about the fact that she had a man in her house who was in the Volunteers and she said to Mrs. Keeffe, 'who have you to fight for Ireland only old Bacchus', a reference to the fact that Mrs. Keeffe's husband had at one time been over fond of the drop. And she said to Mrs. Dowling, 'who have you to fight for Ireland only the one handed man'. The elder of Mrs. Dowling's two sons had no use in one of his hands. She didn't say anything to my mother, for my father was dead, and my brothers were only children. She then departed and went into her own house, where she hung out through the window, where she still kept up a string of abuse. Mrs. Keeffe said if she came into her again she would throw a bucket of water over her. At last the string of abuse ceased, and there was silence for a while. We children were dancing around the footpath outside her house, waiting to see what would happen next, for it was a bit of excitement in our uneventful lives.

The next sound we heard was moaning inside the hall door. Nobody could do anything, for they could not get in. At last John Lawlor arrived and found Molly lying on the floor at the foot of the stairs. he came in for my mother and together they managed to get her upstairs, and John threw her upon the bed as if she was a sack of meal, saying, 'she is a hopeless case'. Somebody sent for a doctor, and Molly was brought to the Infirmary, where they diagnosed a broken hip. She was there for several months, and thereafter always walked with the aid of a stick, and one of her legs was shorter than the other. I think that what my mother and John Lawlor did would not happen today. They moved her not knowing that if she had been left there until a doctor was called, and she had been gently lifted on to a stretcher, and brought by ambulance to hospital, she would not have had one leg shorter than the other. Every pay day afterwards she stayed in bed and Pat brought in her drink to her. I don't remember how long this went on for, but one Christmas morning when my mother was coming home from six o'clock Mass, there was an ambulance outside Butler's door and Pat's dead body was being brought out on a stretcher. He had been drinking in Matt Keeffe's pub for most of Christmas Eve and Matt was trying to get him home and promised he would give him, what I suppose one would call 'a cure', if he came down on Christmas morning. Molly and John Lawlor lived on together for a few years, then tragedy struck again. John came home one night after having a few drinks. He told Molly he was very hungry. Molly cooked him a meal of rashers and eggs and sausages, and shortly afterwards he got a severe pain. The doctor was sent for, but he died before morning. As with Pat's death, the general belief among the neighbours was, they had both smothered their hearts with too much drink. Molly lived on alone for several years, then went into a home for old people, where she eventually died.

Chapter 2

Poverty, St Kevin and Sunday Evenings

My mother married again, about three years after my father's death. He was another tailor by trade, and it came about in this way. His name was Davy Murphy, and he was a widower and was old enough to be my mother's father. He lived on our row of houses, in number 33. He lived on his own, next door to his married daughter and his two grown up sons lived with her. One day a policeman called on him, and gave him twenty four hours to vacate his house, so that a member of the Black and Tans could move into it. The Black and Tans were an Auxiliary Force set up to help the British Army. His daughter came and asked my mother if she would rent our sitting room to her father as a workroom. My mother was only too glad to rent the room as she had the large amount of thirteen shillings weekly to keep six of us, and out of this she had to pay three and sixpence weekly for rent. At one time she went to a Corporation member, in fact I think he was the Mayor at the time, Peter Deloughry (he was the man who made the key which got de Valera out of Lincoln Gaol) to ask if he could get the rent reduced a little for her. All the help he gave her was to ask if she could get a smaller house. My mother replied that she hoped to have her family reared some day. There were six of us in a house with three bedrooms, and one of them no bigger than a box room. After that my mother took in washing to help to feed us and I will never forget the appearance of the kitchen when we came home from school, with the bath up against the kitchen table and my mother scrubbing away against the washboard.

It must have been extra hard on my mother for she had never gone out to work before her marriage, she being the younger of two girls by six years. Her sister, whose name was Mary Ellen, served her apprenticeship as a dressmaker, but never worked at it afterwards, for she hated it and she went into domestic service instead. She was a quiet gentle person, and our dearly loved Auntie, for that is what we always called her. My father's brother and his family lived at the other side of the city, in Gaol Street, and

13

we were never close to them. We visited constantly the family of my father's first cousin, the Loughman's of New Street. The sons of this family all fought in the War of Independence, and one of them, the eldest daughter Maggie, paid dearly for it. During the Civil War she was bringing his dinner over to one of her brothers who was stationed in the Military Barracks on the Castlecomer Road when she was shot in her thigh by a sniper's bullet, and she had to have her leg amputated from above her knee. I would think that it took all the joy out of life for her, for she could never wear an artificial limb, she got around on crutches. She was only in her early twenties and a very pretty girl. She never married, which probably she would have done only for her handicap.

I have digressed a bit here for I should have explained further about our Lodger. My mother was seemingly very happy in her second marriage, but our money difficulties were far from over, for although my stepfather gave her every penny he earned, some weeks he might not get even one suit to make, and that left us penniless, and now and again he might make two suits, and when one of us children delivered them we might be told, 'I'll pay for them next week'. This meant, that one of us would have to go down to Matt Keeffe's, the grocery shop in John Street; and ask for the groceries on 'tick', as we called on credit.

The poverty of those days was frightening, and I have never forgotten it. But if times were hard we children were always able to amuse ourselves. We played what we called beds, on the wide footpath outside our houses. We marked out with chalk six divisions, and placed a bit of slate, or smooth stone on number one, and standing on one foot moved the stone from one to six with the other foot, that is, if we didn't move the stone outside the chalked sections, then we would be out. We also played rounders on the road, which consisted of placing four large stones at an equal distance apart, and one of each team in their turn hit the ball in the direction of the opposing team. If the ball was caught by one of the opposing team then it was their turn to play. We always dreaded having Fanny Connolly against us, for she was a big strong girl, and could hit the ball nearly to the end of the street. In the Summer we gave most of our free time paddling in the river, the Nore of course, down on the Quay. The boys all used to go swimming, but we girls were content just to go paddling, just walking about in the river with our dresses pulled up to our knees, and tucked into the elastic bands at the end of our knickers which came down to our knees in those days. We also caught what we called brickaleens, in glass jars to which we tied a length of twine. We would bring them home and empty them into an old basin, and feed them with bits of weeds. Of course they eventually died. I think its only we Irish children who called the small fish brickaleens, in the dictionary they are called tiddlers.

The boys used also go swimming in a place called Garranascrean. We

14

girls never went there. I think it was a fairly good distance outside the city, and one went out the Hebron Road to it. One Saturday when Jack and his friends were swimming there, he stood on a broken bottle and cut the sole of his foot. Jack limped home as best he could with the blood pouring from his foot. I don't know why my mother didn't send for the doctor, maybe she was afraid he would give out to her on account of it being a Saturday evening (In those days people were scared out of their wits of doctors, poor people were at any rate.). Anyway, my mother washed and bandaged Jack's foot, and I cannot remember whether she brought him over to the Dispensary on the Monday morning or if she sent for the doctor to come to the house, but when he examined Jack's foot he told my mother that if he had seen his foot immediately it would have needed five stitches, but he could not stitch it then. Jack limped for several weeks with an upturned sweeping brush under his arm for a crutch. If it happened now he would be loaned crutches from the Clinic. So much for the 'good old days'.

We always discussed the price of all sweets before we bought them. One day we were outside Ellen Rafter's shop in John Street, and we were discussing the price of oranges in the window. One of our group said, 'I bet they are about three ha-pence each', so Essie Flynn volunteered to go in and ask the price. In walked Essie, and said to Ellen, 'how much are the three ha-penny oranges in the window'. 'If you don't get out quick' says Ellen, 'I'll give you three ha-penny oranges'. She thought that Essie was trying to be smart, but she wasn't, but she kind of had three ha-penny sweets on the brain, we had said it so many times. To go back to my stepfather, he was always nice and kind to us but it was very different from having our own father. He would tell yarns, sometimes of the bawdy type and, then my mother would stop him. To an adult nowadays they would be harmless, and some years ago when I read *The Tailor and Ansty*, I thought he was the exact prototype of the Tailor, even in his appearance. One evening when my mother was after reading a poem to us about St. Kevin and Glendalough, he started to tell us why there were seven churches built at Glendalough. He said there was a certain man and his wife lived there and the wife used to give birth to a baby every year. Eventually, the man said he would go away, which he did, as he felt his wife could not rear any more children. After seven years the man returned, and after nine months his wife gave birth to seven babies, all boys. The father decided that no way could they feed seven more children, so he tied them into a sack and went off to drown them. On the way he met a priest who knew him, and the priest said to the father, 'what have you in the sacks, 'pups Father' he answered, 'which I am going to drown'. 'Open the sack' said the priest, which the father did,. 'Bring home those babies and rear them', said the priest. The father did as he was told and the seven boys became Bishops and between them built the Seven Churches at Glendalough. We children loved the poem to Saint Kevin which my mother used to read to us, and which I have remembered through the years.

> By that lake whose gloomy shore,
> Skylark never warbles oe'r
> Where the cliffs hang low
> And steep young Saint Kevin stole to sleep
> Here at least he calmly said
> Women ne'er shall find my bed
> But the good Saint little knew
> What the wily sex can do.
> Twas from Kathleen's eyes he flew
> Eyes of most unholy blue
> She had loved him well and long
> Wished him hers nor thought it wrong.
> Where so ere the Saint did fly,
> Still he heard her light foots nigh
> On the bold cliffs bosom cast
> Tranquil now he sleeps at last.

I often wondered, as a child, was Saint Kevin brought up and charged with her murder, or was the story a myth. I could have learned a lot of Irish history, at first hand from my stepfather but being young and impatient, I listened to only a little of what he said, but one thing which always stayed in my mind was the fact that he was playing with St. John's Band in Castlecomer, on the day that lime was thrown at Parnell. This was after his affair with Kitty O'Shea had become public. Of course he never believed it was true about Kitty O'Shea and Parnell and neither did my mother, although she was not nearly as patriotic as he was. They both blamed the bishops and priests for his downfall.

We children made all our own amusements in those days. We would have concerts in turn in each other's back yards. We opened the concert, and also closed with 'Oft In The Stilly Night'. The charge was one penny, and the proceeds went to have, what we considered a party, which consisted of biscuits and lemonade. During one such concert, which we held in Berry's yard, Moira Berry was in the middle of rendering 'The Boys Stood On The Burning Deck' when suddenly she stopped, and shouted, 'Look at Judy Thompson looking over the wall and she didn't pay at all'. We were never bored, and on the Sundays when we didn't go walking the railway line we used to walk down the Canal Walk or Lacken, where we always went into the tiny building which housed the well, and drank out of the iron cup which was attached to the wall by a chain. We never got any infection from so many people drinking from it.

I have described the kind of lavatory we had in our row of houses. Well,

16

the row lower down than ours which I think were built later than ours had an entry door and a small door behind it through which everything which went through the lavatory was cleaned out a couple of times a week. The man who cleaned them out we called 'Billy Stink', that is, we children called him that, the adults didn't call him this. We would be in bed when we would hear him passing, pushing his hand cart, for he lived in Wolfe Tone Street, which was just around the corner from us.

I can remember just a few people whom we would call 'characters'. Johnathan Buggy, who after hearing a Missioner condemn the Jews for putting our Lord to death went into Saint John's Church and shook his first up at the Stations Of The Cross on the wall and shouted, 'Come down out of that you Christ killers'. Then there was Jim Doheny who was about six feet six inches tall and when a wag said to him one day, 'Hand me down the moon'. Jim replied, 'I would only your ould wan would pawn it'. We all believed in ghosts in those days and in curses being handed down from one generation to another. My mother used to tell us that there was a curse on the head of The House Of Waterford. This was put on them by a widow whose son was hanged, on the order of the then head of the house of Waterford. According to my mother the poor boy was guilty of only a small misdemeanour. The curse was, that for seven generations the head of the family would not die in his bed. In my lifetime three of them have not died in their beds. I believe the curse is finished now. I clearly remember the death of the last Marquis. He went out early one morning with his gun, game shooting I think, but he was later found shot dead. He was a young man, with two young sons.

My mother also told us about a landlord family in Co. Carlow. One of the sons of the family was born without arms or legs. The reason for this my mother told us, was that his mother gave a party before he was born, ordered a pie to be made with the image of the Blessed Mother engraved in pastry on the top. When the pie was brought to the table, she first cut off the arms and legs, and that was the reason that the child she was carrying was born without arms or legs. Nearly all the adults I knew when I was a child firmly believed in ghosts, and we children did too. If we heard any unusual sound in the night it was surely a ghost, and it might be only a cat bawling. Leyrath, about two miles outside the city always had the name of being haunted. My mother used to tell us about the night the man who was driving a wagonette, could not get the horses to go past the gate leading into Leyrath house; he got down off the wagonette and got an awful fright. It was not anything he saw that frightened him, he said but what he walked on. We never knew what it was, but we children would go for a walk out the Dublin Road, but would never pass Leyrath gate.

My grandmother, on my mother's side lived with us, after her husband died, but I do not remember her for she died when I was only two years old.

She was the only girl in her family and had seven brothers, who were all Blacksmiths. I think they lived in the village of Danesfort, some miles outside the city. My mother used to tell us that she was a very gentle woman, and not very talkative, but she always regretted that she hadn't a sister, as every week she had to starch and iron eight white shirt fronts for her father and brothers, and those shirt fronts would be pleated, so it must have been hard tedious work. My mother also told us that if her brothers committed any misdemeanour (I should say here my grandmother's brothers) their mother would complain them to their father in Irish, when he came home after work at night. My grandmother used to say, that Irish people themselves were partly to blame for the Irish language dying out, as if parents spoke it to their children at home it would never have died. My grandmother also used to say that there is a cure in the earth, or I suppose it would be more correct to say the soil, for every disease, if only it could be found. Another thing she used to say was, that one should take off ones hat in homage to spiders for the beautiful webs they spin. This has been brought home to me very forcefully each time I look at television when the National Anthem is being played, when I look at the beautiful webs portrayed on the screen.

There was a great neighbourliness in those days, and hardly a week went by without somebody borrowing a cup of sugar or an egg cup full of tea which was always returned on Saturday. Those who were not so poor were the Dowling's, who lived two doors from us, and the Connolly's who lived four doors down. The Connolly's father had been a sergeant major in the British army, and was retired, so I suppose he had a pension which helped to make them better off than the rest of us. They also kept pigs in the garden, and often I went up to the railway station with Fanny Connolly, the daughter, to collect offal from their Aunt, who worked there as a cook, this was to help feed the pigs. The Connolly's never, or hardly ever, bought a loaf of bread, for one day Sarah Connolly, the eldest daughter said to my mother, 'Mrs. Loughman, I would eat a whole loaf of bought bread if I had it'. My mother used to bake, white soda bread on a big iron pan over the open fire, she would have a couple of bricks on each hob at the side of the open fire, and the pan would be raised over the fire, high enough to keep the bread from burning. The edges of the bread would then be browned in front of the fire. I suppose all housework was equivalent to hard labour when compared to all the labour saving devices we have today. Almost everybody on our row of houses kept hens. They were housed in the coalhouse. Every morning they were let out, and into the field across the road. Opposite our house, which was in the middle of the row, there was an opening cut in the wall through which they went into the field, and there was another opening opposite Fennelly's, which was the first house on the row. When the hens had an egg to lay, they would come out of the field and cross the road and stand outside the door to be let in. They would lay their egg and when we would hear the cackling we would know they had laid their egg, and would let them out again, out through the hall, across the road and into the field. I think the holes are closed now, for I know there were no chickens in the field when I was over there a couple of years ago, and sadly, no children playing on the street.

Another walk we children sometimes took on Sundays was over to the graveyard of St. Canice's Cathedral (the church was always locked, so we were never in it), and what fascinated us about the graveyard was, the figure of a child, I don't know if it was meant to be an angel, over the grave of the child of the Bell family of Kilcreene. They were, I would imagine what we would call ascendancy, and the head of the family was Master of the foxhounds for many years. I can well remember going over with my friends to see the guests arriving for the wedding of a member of the Poe family, a very grand affair. Looking back on this what remains in my memory most forcefully is, the members of the Loftus family, who were Catholics, walking up and down outside in their wedding finery waiting for the wedding party to come out, for they dare not go into the church for the ceremony under pain of mortal sin, or maybe excommunication. The awful bigotry of it did not strike any of us at the time, for we thought that anybody who wasn't a Catholic was damned. Every Sunday afternoon at about two-thirty the pupils from Kilkenny College, which is situated in John Street would come up Michael Street in two's and three's. They would be dressed in black and white striped trousers, short cutaway black jackets, I think they are called "Eton jackets', stiff white collars, and 'Mortar Board Hats', I think they would be on their way to afternoon Service in Saint Canice's Cathedral. They belonged to the Church of Ireland. This College can of course claim the credit of being the Alma Mater of at least two famous men, Swift and Berkeley.

There was one Protestant family on our street, the Cleere family. There were several girls, and only one boy. Their father was dead, but most of the girls were older than our age group, so I suppose they were working, for they seemed to be able to live fairly well. Eva was the youngest girl, and sometimes used to play with us, but our play often ended in a row, a verbal one, and we would shout at her:

> Proddy Woddy on the wall,
> A half a loaf will do ye all.
> A penny candle will show ye light
> To pick a bone on Friday night

Eva would reply:

> Catholic, catholic go to Mass
> Riding on the devil's ass.

They lived on the row of houses below us, and we never knew their mother very well, but my mother used to say she was a very neighbourly woman to those near her. This we found difficult to believe, for we, poor misguided children, thought there was no such person as a good neighbourly Protestant. Most of the time while I was growing up there was political unrest. We used to see the Black and Tans driving by with a helpless hostage in their lorries, tenders they used to call the vehicles. The poor victim used to be bound hand and foot, and he might not have anything to do with the Republic army, but he helped to keep them, the Tans, safe from attack, as the Republicans could not risk shooting one of their own countrymen. We in the city were comparatively safe from house raids by the Tans, but the people in rural areas were the ones who suffered from raids on their homes, as it was they, especially in remote areas who sheltered men. My stepfather used to say that the R.I.C. men were more guilty than the Tans, for it was they who led the Tans to what were considered safe houses, they knew the lie of the land and the Tans did not, and they were able to stand aside and let the Tans murder and loot at will. I think I have said before now that we were not a patriotic family, but during the 1914 war when the British spoke of bringing in conscription eventually a spark of patriotism emerged in my mother, and she was vociferous in her condemnation of it. Mrs. Keeffe, our next door neighbour was equally so, and with more reason, for her only son was old enough to be conscripted, and she did not see why her dearly loved son should have to fight in a war which was none of our making. My brothers were too young to be conscripted. The only person who was in favour of it, was a Mrs. Loughran, who lodged in a house at the top of our row, and whose husband was already in the British army, and she had, what everybody called then, Separation Money. She had no children. One day she came into our house and she held forth loud and long on the advantages of men joining the British Army. Mrs. Keeffe came in and she was not long in silencing Mrs. Loughran. Mrs. Keeffe was a very intelligent well read woman, and was well able to tell her all the disadvantages of doing so. I was just four years old when the 1916 Rising took place, and the only significance it had for me, until I grew up and read Irish history for myself was 'there was no bread in Dublin for a week'.

Chapter 3

More memories of the Marble City

I went to the Presentation Convent from the lake school when I was about ten years old. I did not like the nuns, for in general they were snobs, all of them, or almost all, favoured farmer's daughters and shopkeepers' daughters. Especially favoured was a girl named Cissie Fennel. She lived in Welling Square with her two aunts and an uncle. Her uncle was the manager of Lipton's, but Cissie was perfect in the opinion of all the nuns. I know she never failed to answer any question she was asked, but I do not think that was why the nuns made such a fuss of her, I think it was because the job her uncle had was considered grand in those days. I was supposed to be brainy too, but I often missed answering my lessons. Maybe it was because I was often kept at home from school, because my mother was always ailing. My school days were a nightmare. I think I went into the Secondary School for about one year, but I am not too clear in my memory about this.

One priceless gift God has given me, and that is, a love of reading. I started with Ethel M. Dells, *The Way of An Eagle.*Ursula Bloom's novelettes, all light reading. *The Way Of An Eagle* has stayed in my minds more clearly than any other book which I read in my youth. I thought, what a hero the main male character in the book was, Nick Ratcliffe was his name, and he risked life and limb as a British Spy for his glorious Empire. In my ignorance, I though he was a wonderful person, and that all the Indians were murderers. Mrs. Henry Wood's *East Lynne*, was a book I read more than once. I think it was my favourite of all the books I read during my childhood. I never read any of the classics until I was into my teens. All the books I read were borrowed from the Library on John's Quay. When my mother would send me upstairs to sweep the bedrooms I'd always bring a book up with me. I'd sweep for a while then I'd sit on a bed and read a bit. Every now and then I'd give the floor a bang of the sweeping brush. After a while I'd forget to bang, and my mother would shout up, 'what are you doing up there so long', so that would finish my reading until evening.

To mention again what Christmas meant to us as children, the first sign of it was the light in the big long shed in the Market Yard, which signified that the plucking of turkeys had begun. Most of the women who could do with a few extra shillings for Christmas would be there plucking the turkeys for the payment of three pence per bird. I don't know who they worked for directly, but the birds would appear in the shops in time for Christmas. The shed in the Market yard was also used on Saturdays, all the year round, by farmer's wives selling butter. They would sit in a row on forms with baskets of butter on their laps. The rolls would be of different weights, and would usually be on leafs of cabbage. The housewives would go from one to another tasting the butter. They would lift off a bit, either with a sixpenny bit, or their thumb. If the taste wasn't to their liking they would keep going from one to the other until they found a taste to their liking. The lowest price I remember butter being was ten pence per pound. I think they sold eggs too but we never bought them there.

One of the dearest wishes as a child was to be allowed to strew rose petals in front of the Blessed Eucharist during the processions. One was held in our Parish of Saint John, on the feast of Corpus Christi, and one each Sunday evening during the month of May, in the grounds of The Black Abbey. My mother brought me to them all, but my ambition was never realised. I have said that none of our neighbours ever called each other by their Christian names, but always Mrs, but it was different with the men, they were Pat, and Jim, and John, which were the names of most of our male neighbours. My mother had one friend from her school days with whom she was on Christian name terms. She lived in 'Maudlin Street', and she usually brought one of her daughters with her when she visited us each week. Her name was Nell Walsh, and she was my mother's closest friend. Her husband Ned, worked at Collis's stoneyards, which were situated a few miles outside the city, to which he walked each day. Nell was a very well spoken intelligent woman, and very proud of her husband's craft, for to this day, over the span of a lifetime, I can hear her words ringing in my ears. She would say to my mother 'Katie, you know Ned is not a stone cutter, he is a marblemason'.

Mrs. Walsh was also very patriotic, and her proud boast was, that her father was a Fenian. My mother and I, also visited at her house every week, and I listened to the conversations, but I hardly ever spoke. We always tried to get home before twelve o'clock, for we were all very superstitious in those days and firmly believed in ghosts, and that they didn't appear until after twelve o'clock.

22

I can remember going down to Walsh's when Sinn Fein won in the nineteen eighteen election and seeing a bonfire burning on top of the castle in Maudlin Street to celebrate their victory. I have read lately that the castle, as we called it was originally a 'Leper Settlement'. Some people even believed there was a green white and yellow band around the moon on the night of the election. The first aeroplane to fly over Kilkenny must have been during the 1914-18 war. I remember the graphic description of it my mother gave in after years. The pilot's name was Corbett Wilson, he was an officer in the British Air Force, and lived in a place called Ardaloo in County Kilkenny I think. He flew right in front of our houses, over the river and looped the loop several times. My father was leaning on the wall opposite our house clapping, and my mother was in the kitchen with a lighted Blessed Candle in her hand, for she thought the pilot's last hour had come. He flew back home safely however. He had a man-servant who composed a poem in his honour, and the words of which I learned from my mother:

> God bless you Corbett Wilson,
> May your courage never fail.
> May a hundred years pass over
> Till your coffin needs a nail.
> May the grace of God go with you,
> And see you safely through.
> To give us all another show
> Some day at Ardaloo.

I don't know if he gave another show at Ardaloo, but he did not come over the city again, for he was killed in action during the war. Another exciting day in our lives was the Sunday when Kilkenny would be playing in the All Ireland hurling final. We had no radio in those days, but the Murray family of Wolfe Tone Street had carrier pigeons, and around six o'clock a crowd gathered there awaiting the return of the pigeons with the results of the matches, for sometimes Kilkenny might have two teams playing — Minor, as well as Senior. The first person to have a radio on our street was Tom Dowling. He lived in the row of houses next to ours. It was called Abbey View Terrace. The houses were owned by a man named Healy, who had a public house in John Street. I always thought that the residents of this Terrace thought they were superior to us who paid rent to the Corporation. Be that as it may, everybody who could fit into Dowling's kitchen was welcome on the day of an All Ireland. It was never called the hurling final, but always the All Ireland. If the match was a close one Tom would be out in the yard, and would shout in through the window every now and again, 'who's winning lads'. He couldn't bear the the tension of listening directly.

The late Francis McManus was reared on our street. I don't know if any of his family were born on it but he, and his two brothers, and only sister whose name was May were there as long as I can remember. He was never called Francis in those days, but Paddy. His father died when they were all young, and, what was most unusual in those days their mother got his job as a commercial traveller.

They had a housekeeper who practically reared them for their mother's work kept her away from home, except for weekends. Paddy was a quiet studious type of boy. We hadn't much contact with them, for they lived near the end of the street, whereas we lived near the top, and I think they spent all the school holidays with relatives in the country. The clearest memory of them is my envy of May's ownership of a scooter, on which she gave me a ride now and again. It was only two pieces of timber, one to which to small wheels were attached, and another upright piece, with two small handles. One put one's foot on the flat piece, and the other on the ground, with which one propelled the scooter. It was one of the ambitions of my childhood to own a scooter, an ambition which was never realised, for the biggest toy which my mother could afford was a small doll, and that only at Christmas.

I was never farther outside the city than I could walk. I think the village of Dunmore was the only village in the country I, and my friends ever visited. One of our favourite walks on Sundays was down the Bishops Meadows as far as Talbots Inch, and there we would give a long time looking at the residents (at least I think they were all residents who played there) playing tennis, a game which none of us could ever see ourselves playing, for we thought it was only for rich people. Still, we were happy, as we wound our way homeward in time for our tea. We nearly always had homemade bread, and an apple or rhubarb tart, according to the season. When Jack was barely into his teens he went to work as a pantry boy at the Club House Hotel, and from pantry boy to waiter. At the Club House Hotel, Anew McMaster stayed every year, when his Company came to Kilkenny, for one week. Jack used to have long conversations with him, mostly about acting, for it was the greatest ambition of his life to be a Shakespearean actor. He could recite passages from Shakespeare's plays and strike a pose as if he was on the stage.

Anew McMaster used to get him to scrub his back in the bath, on the nights when he would be playing Othello, and Jack managed to see most of the plays during the week. He was always talking of another male member of the Company, who promised him that he would get him into the Company to study to be an actor. One year after they left

Kilkenny he wrote to Jack, who showed the letter to my mother, who read it, and then put it in the fire and forbade Jack to have anything further to do with this man. It was only when I grew up and found out there were such people as homosexuals, that I realised why my mother acted as she did. I never knew this man's name, but Jack used to say he was very tall and handsome. Jack was only of medium height, but was exceedingly handsome, but I think now, in a feminine way.

Poor as we were my mother always managed to have enough money to bring Billy and myself to the plays, some of them at any rate. We never missed *Hamlet, The Merchant of Venice*, and *The Bells*. When the D'Oley Carte Opera Company came we went to *Maritana, The Bohemian Girl* and *Carmen*. I do not know a lot about my father's family. I know that when my parents were married, they lived at No. 35 Maudlin Street, which house, I believe, with No. 34, once was the residence of the priests of St. John's Parish. My father had many brothers and sisters. The only two who lived in Kilkenny were my father and his brother Dick whom I have already mentioned. Two girls of the family worked in England, Mary and Kate. The other members of the family to the best of my knowledge emigrated to America. When I was still very young this woman appeared at our door one day with her three daughters and my brother Jack by the hand. She had met him down John Street and recognised him from a family likeness. She chided my mother for Jack being barefoot, but my mother told her that almost all the boys on our street went barefoot in the summer. The woman was my Aunt Mary and she lived in London, and had three sons and three daughters, and had married an Irishman, one of the Fennessy family from Clonmel. They had a shoe-shop in O'Connell Street. Their eldest daughter Molly worked in the English civil service and when the Treaty of 1921 was signed she came to work in Dublin on an exchange basis. From that time onwards my Aunt Mary kept in touch with my mother and sent us her daughter's cast off clothes, which as I got older fitted me and which we were very glad to get.

My mother told me, that when the Irish delegation went over to London for the Treaty negotiations in 1921, my aunt Mary broke out of the crowd outside Downing Street, and ran over and embraced Michael Collins, and sure enough, when R.T.E. showed Robert Kee's documentary, on our fight for Independence a couple of years ago, I watched closely, and saw the woman going over to Collins. Unless one knew of it, it would not mean anything to the ordinary watcher, for the movement of the cameras was swift, and the pictures shadowy. My eldest son, who unfortunately had to leave Ireland as he could not get work at home rang me from Plymouth, where he now lives to tell me that he too had seen it. My aunt Mary's eldest son was one of those who carried the coffin of Terence McSwiney out of Brixton Prison. My aunt Mary seemed to be very well off, for she came over on holidays with her daughters, as far as I can remember several years in succession, which was surprising for a widow, for there were no widow's pensions in those days, and it must have cost a fair amount of money. Her late husband had worked in the English civil service. I am sure she had a pension as his widow but I don't think she could have lived as she did without having another source of income.

I did not know my father had another sister until I went to work in England. It happened like this. One day my mother met one of the Loughman's who lived in New Street. It was one of the girls. My mother mentioned to her that I had gone to work in England. She asked my mother what part of England, and she told her it was in Woodmansterne in Surrey not far from where Kate lived, so she gave her my address. Shortly after this I had a letter from Aunt Kate inviting me to her home on my next day off.

She lived with her husband in Thornton Heath, and when she answered my letter she gave me a description of her person, and said she would be holding a white handkerchief in her hand. I had no trouble in recognising her. After this visit I went to her, on my day off once a month, and she also told me to bring one of the girls who worked with me, which I did, and she and her husband always gave us a great welcome. Her husband was an Englishman, a lovely gentle man. They had no children, and were all in all to each other. My father's other sister Mary eventually settled in Dublin, I never saw any of her three sons. I think this Aunt was a bit of a snob and a social climber, for she never looked up any of the friends she knew in her childhood in Kilkenny. There was a Mrs. McHugh who lived in a small house at the end of Michael Street, and although I was only a child at the time, I remember she giving out to me about her, and saying she was too grand to talk to her old friends. But maybe I am wronging her in describing her thus, for she had been a long time out of Ireland, and the years may have dimmed her memory. She was very good to us, and I ought not to forget it. She also heard I was working in England and one day she called to Lloyd's house to see me and invited me to her home which was at the other side of London. She gave me one bit of advice which I don't think I heeded and it was 'Don't ever get your photograph taken in servant's uniform'. The reason for this was that I might 'come up in the world', is the only way I can phrase it and I wouldn't want anyone to know I had been a domestic servant.

All my life I have come up against this class consciousness. Firstly, when I was a child, Mrs. Kerwick who lived in the row of houses next to ours, and whose husband was an attendant (called a male nurse now) in the Mental Hospital, used to keep bank clerks as lodgers, or I might be more correct in saying boarders, for they were given their meals as well as their bed. They all wore plusfours, and walked up and down the street as removed from us as if they came from another planet. Then there was the Quinn's father. They lived second next door to us. He was a painting contractor and his sons, when they were old enough worked with him. He never mixed with any of the men on our street but with solicitors and professional men. We could always go into Quinn's when only their mother was at home. She was a lovely motherly woman, and a great neighbour, but if we children knocked at the door when the father was at home we would be told at the door in hushed tones 'Me father is at home'. An exception to this was, at the beginning of the salmon fishing season, when almost always, on the first day of the season, their father would catch a salmon. We would all be let in to admire the salmon, and as it was almost always a very large fish, we would look at it in awe, and admire it. The father would always be there then, and be very nice to us.

The Flynn family lived two doors above us, and their father used to tell about the executions which were carried out on John's Green. They did not take place during his lifetime, but he had a photograph of two men who had witnessed an execution. Executions were always by hanging in those days. In the photograph, the men were small and dwarflike, and they looked simple. Anyway, one day a neighbour went into the house and was just in time to avert a tragedy. In many Irish homes at that time, and even in my childhood, people had fairly large hooks hanging from their ceilings, mostly to hang half of a pig's head from, so that they could absorb the smoke which came from the open fire. Underneath this hook, the brothers had the kitchen table, and on the table one of the brothers was standing, with a rope around his neck, which rope attached to the hook in the ceiling, the other brother was shouting at him 'kick, damn your soul you have the knack'. Whether he would have hanged or not is debatable, but Mr. Flynn was sure he would have, only for the intervention of the neighbour.

Every year we had a fortnight's mission. One week for the men and one week for the women. I used to dread it, for the missioners used to put the fear of God into anyone who was anyway scrupulous. I was only a child and I used to be terrified. My mother and her sister, our auntie, were always nervous wrecks by the time it was over. They would go to confession, after queuing, usually for hours. They would come home fairly happy, and then they would begin to think they didn't make a good confession, and back they would go again. I often think that the missions made more nervous wrecks of people than the hardships they had to endure in those days. A priest once said to my mother that missions don't have any effect on those who they are meant for, but they upset timid scrupulous people, and no wonder they did, for seldom did they speak of the love and mercy of God. They thundered mostly about sins against the sixth commandment, and courting couples going out the lonely roads, and my stepfather used to say, 'where else would they go, did you ever see a man kissing a girl under a lamp post'. My stepfather had the awful habit of interspersing the Holy Name in every sentence he uttered. My mother was always on to him about it, but to no avail. It had become second nature to him, but one day he went to confession to one of the priests of our parish, a Father Cavanagh. He was a very retiring, haughty looking man, but a very good priest. He knew every one of his parishioners. Anyway, when my stepfather confessed to his misuse of the Holy Name, he gave him a lecture, and wound up by saying, 'If God struck you dumb what would you do', and from that day, to the day he died I never heard him say it again.

There used to be dozens of people going to confession, and one might have to wait maybe a couple of hours before one could be heard. I remember on a couple of occasion s 'holding' a seat for Nan Keeffe, our next door neighbour. This involved going over to the church, St. John's church, maybe an hour or two hours before Nan got off from work. When she came I would get up and give her my place. There were always forms placed along the wall at each side of the confession box during the Mission. The main body of pentinents would be in the usual pews of the church, and as each person from the forms went into the confession box one would come out from the pew and take their place at the end of the form. I must have been in my early teens at the time, and had left school. Nan used to reward me in some way but whether it was money or a present I cannot remember.

I should have finished what I had to say about the sins against the sixth commandment, before I rambled on about my stepfather. The following will bear out what I have said about the priests' obsession with that sin. In the small town where I have lived for the past fifty years, there was one such mission. One night, after the mission devotions were over, a bachelor farmer went into a certain pub in the town, and when he had ordered his drink said to the owner of the pub who was behind the counter, 'Do you know what Mrs. ......, there's no sin in Ireland only the ould sthunt', and he was right.

In the Winter we children never missed the coursing, on Sundays at any rate. It was held on Hanrahan's land at Altamount. Not realising that it was a cruel barbarous sport, we only walked around and enjoyed the crowd and excitement. I was only a child when I realised that anticipation is nearly always better than reality. About twice a week, Kitty Quinn, Kathleen Geoghegan and myself would go up the Dublin

28

Road to Wilson's of Lacken for a 'sweet gallon' full of separated milk, for our mothers to make bread with. We would stop several times on our way back, and scoop with our fingers the froth from the top of the milk. I thought for a long time, wouldn't it be a lot nicer if I could spoon it, so one day I brought a teaspoon. 'Did it taste nicer? 'Not a bit of it'. It was much nicer from my fingers. My mother bore one child from her second marriage — a boy, Michael. My brother, Billy, always believed that she loved Michael better than all the rest of us, and I think he was right. He was kept at school longer than the rest of us, and my mother never expected any help financially from him, which she did from the rest of us. Billy went to work in the Newspaper Office at the Railway station when he left school. This entailed being on the platform with newspapers and magazines, when the trains came in. I think that he had to deliver them to certain houses as well. When he got too old for that job he went, like Jack to work in the Club House Hotel.

I often wondered would things have been different, if my father had to live, would my brothers have had better jobs. I think they would, for my father would have had a secure job and I think he would have ambitions for us. The boys would have had a trade although I know that to a great many people a trade is nothing to be proud of. To me it is, and I think it was Shakespeare who wrote 'He who has a trade has an estate'. What brings it home to me more forcefully is when I think of the neighbour whom I have already mentioned, Jimmy Flynn. He was a fitter, and worked for the gas works. My mother said he was illiterate, and only for that he would have been a manager, but he was brilliant at his trade, and several times each year he would go up to Belfast to do work that nobody else was capable of doing. Paddy was the only one of my brothers who had a trade but it didn't do him much good for the minute he was finished serving his time, Stathams let him go. They didn't want to pay him a man's wages. He was then only sixteen years of age. He looked more, for he was then six feet tall, and was built in proportion, and by the time he was twenty, he was six feet two inches, and as fine a man as you would see anywhere. He was kind and gentle, as were all my brothers. Paddy was several months at home and couldn't get a job, so in the end he joined the Army, in the Transport corps, so I suppose his trade did stand to him in the end. I can remember him going with the rest of Statham's staff to see the 'bleeding statues' in Templemore. I think they went by wagonette, but what stays in my mind most forcefully is the frightening belief we had in ghosts, and if they were late coming back, how would Paddy pass St. Maul's graveyard. We children could always visualise a figure emerging from a graveyard dressed completely in white, from head to feet, and with arms outstretched. My stepfather used to say to us, with great commonsense 'Firstly, you believe in God, in heaven, hell and purgatory'. 'Well', he'd say 'If you go to hell, you know you will never get out of it'. 'If you go to purgatory you can't get out until you are cleansed of your sins, then you will go to heaven, and that's such a lovely place you won't want to get out of it'. Good logic, but we were still afraid of ghosts.

Weddings in the days of my youth were lovely homely family affairs (that would be just relatives who lived in the same area) and neighbourly celebrations. The only gloomy part of them was the hour the ceremony had to take place. Almost always before eight o'clock Mass in the morning, and on a winter's morning this wasn't very cheering. However, when the wedding breakfast got under way, and a few drinks were served — whiskey usually for the adults, and lemonade for the children — there is no wedding reception these days which could come near it for homeliness and neighbourliness. The breakfast was served in the parlour, with the women friends helping to prepare and bring it from the kitchen. The bride usually wore a costume, which to the people of my childhood meant a coat and skirt, and of course a hat. The bridesmaid was similarly dressed, and there was never more than one. After the breakfast there were a few words of thanks spoken to all assembled by the groom. After that, anybody with any kind of a voice at all would sing a song.

My mother told us that at her wedding my father sang Thomas Moore's beautiful song 'Believe Me If All Those Endearing Young Charms'. She said he had a very good tenor voice, and amid all the troubles of her married life the memory of that song stayed with her.

> Believe me if all those endearing young charms
> Which I gaze on so fondly today.
> Were to change by tomorrow and fleet in my arms
> Like fairy gifts fading away
> Thou would still be adored at this moment thou art
> Let thy loveliness fade as it will
> And around the dear ruin each wish of my heart
> Would entwine itself verdantly still.

I would say that my mother was beautiful in her youth, for she had large blue grey eyes and high cheek bones, which, even in old age gave her a distinguished look. She had several maxims, the chief and most important was, 'you can save yourself from a rogue but you can't from a liar'. Another of her sayings was, 'debt is the worst kind of poverty', and yet another, 'you can do without your own, but you can't do without your neighbour', and no matter what differences there are between

Irish neighbours, if one is in trouble, the difference is forgotten. Likewise, we share in our neighbours' joys, I think, more than any other nation, and nobody has shown this trait in our nature more forcefully than Kickham in his immortal *Knocknagow*.

The supper would not be a late meal, with us at any rate, our last meal would be our tea at around six o'clock. This would be just bread and butter and jam, usually mixed fruit jam, which was the cheapest. I think it must have been during the war, the 1914 to 1916 one. There was no jam to be got, and I used to have brown sugar on my bread. Even today, which is a long long way away from my childhood, I always have to have honey, jam, or marmalade on my bread, otherwise I would not eat more than half a slice of bread. But to go back to my childhood, and the brown sugar. I used to say 'I want a bit of bread, the top crust, a thin bit, brown sugar, and I'll spread it meself'. My brothers used to tease me unmercifully about it when I got older, and also about a dream I had one night, although I suppose it would be more correct to call it a nightmare. There was a small landing in our house, at almost the top of the stairs, you turned on it and went up three more steps. I dreamt that when I started to go up the stairs, on the small landing stood a woman clothed all in black — black coat, black stockings, a black sailor hat, and two long black plaits of hair, having one at each side, over her shoulders, at the front. When I told of my dream at the breakfast next morning one of my brothers said that was Annie Laurie. For months afterwards they would tease me and say, 'did you see any sign of Annie Laurie last night Mary'. I couldn't see anything funny in it for to me, it was a terrifying vision, and for a long long time I would stand at the end of the stairs, afraid to go up, in case the woman in black would suddenly appear. It took years for me to stop being afraid of her, and now, sixty years after, I can see her as plain as if it was yesterday it happened. It was no wonder we were afraid of dreams, and of ghosts, for the adults were always talking about them, and the banshee, who would be heard keening when certain families were going to die. I don't think that the children of today would even listen to such stories, for they have radios and television, and however much adults may give out about children listening and viewing too much, I think the generation in which I grew up, was far from healthy, emotionally.

St. Patrick's Day was a big day in our lives for we would be all looking forward to viewing the big procession which marched through the city. We would congregate at the end of Michael Street to watch it going up John Street. There would be bands, and the members of the men's confraternity would march with a religious banner, behind the first band. Our men's confraternity was dedicated to the Holy Family. I don't remember the names of the other three parish confraternities. The leaders of the procession were the children from the two orphanages in the city Saint Joseph's and Saint Patrick's. The girls would have dark dresses and white pinafores and the boys dark suits, with knee length pants, and round hard white collars. Thanks be to God the days of branding people in this way are over. When the procession was over we would go back up our own street, and we usually wound up the day by playing on the street, or in the field which I have already mentioned, and we would chant,

> Saint Patrick's Day is a very good day.
> We'll kick the Protestants out of the way.
> And when they get under,
> We'll kick them asunder
> Hip, hip for the Catholics
> Hip, hip hooray.

It was only when I got older and went out into the world that I realised the awfulness of our bigotry. At the same time as we derided them, we thought they were superior to us. I suppose this was because they were always well dressed, and kept themselves to themselves. So too it was with country people, but the difference with them was, we really thought they were inferior. County mugs we called them, but if we had any sense we would have realised from the way the nuns treated them at school, they could buy and sell the lot of us, and almost all the nuns were farmer's daughters, for they were the only people who could afford the money which had to be paid when a girl entered a convent. It was supposed to be God who gave them their vocation, but if He gave it to a poor girl she had not a chance of realising it, unless she went on the Foreign Missions.

When I came to live in this rural area over fifty years ago, I realised that a farmhouse, however rundown and shabby it might be, was far superior to any cottage, however well kept that might be. And when country people speak of 'the home place', even though they have been married for many years, they mean the house and farm where they were born. People who were born in labourer's cottages, never refer to their former homes in these terms. Snobbery is very slow to die out in Ireland.

32

Chapter 4

Religion, Poetry and Talbot's Inch

So far I have not said anything much about my maternal grandparents. I know that my grandmother on this side was very gentle, and of a retiring nature, whereas my grandfather was outgoing and restless. At one time, in my mother's youth, he owned a jarvey car, and these were mostly used to meet travellers at the railway station, and bring them to a hotel, or maybe the travellers would be visiting relatives. However, he gave this up after a while, and set sail for America with my grandmother, my mother, and Auntie. They went to Chicago. My mother used to say they weren't half way across the Atlantic before he was sorry. They stayed there for only two years, and then came home again. All my mother ever said about America was, that, if you left a glass of water in your bedroom at night, it would be frozen solid in the morning. My grandfather then worked in Paddy O'Connell's pork and bacon shop at the end of High Street. It is still there, with the name of Dore over it. I think my mother did not experience poverty until she got married, for if she did she would have spoken of it, for poverty leaves an indelible mark on anybody who has experienced it. I have a photograph of my grandfather, and if he was a rich man, going to a Court Function he couldn't have been better dressed. He was, according to my mother's description of him, a fine figure of a man. He was over six feet tall. In the photo, he is dressed in what was called in my young days, a swallow-tailed coat, in a dark colour, a lighter shade of trousers, a waistcoat with a watch chain across it, a white shirt, with what I think one would call a winged collar, a white handkerchief in his coat pocket, a bowler hat, with gloves folded, and both held in his left hand and his right hand holding a walking cane. He had one sister named Ellen, and she worked as a priest's housekeeper. She was a small gentle person, and my mother and Auntie always referred to her between themselves as, 'the lady'. When I was born she wrote to my mother and told her to always dress me in white because I was a girl. I was lucky to be dressed in any colour at all. My mother's father died when the eldest of us, Paddy, was six months old. My grandmother woke up one morning and found him dead in the bed beside her. My mother used to tell us how my grandfather, when Paddy was only a few weeks old, used to walk around the kitchen with a lighted candle in his hand to see if he would notice it. First babies always bring an extra special joy with them. Auntie, my mother's sister, was Paddy's Godmother, and she bought him his Christening Robe, which three days ago, and almost seventy nine years later, was worn by my tenth grandchild, a girl, at her christening.

Of course in my young days everyone 'dealt' at their favourite grocery shop. We 'dealt' at Matt Keeffe's shop in John Street, just at the end of Michael Street and around the corner from it. At Christmas time all the customers got a fine Christmas present, which was a bottle of whiskey, a bottle of Port, a pound of brown sugar (presumably to make punch with the whiskey), a pound of rice, and an Oxford lunch cake. There were two brothers, Matt and Kieran. Matt was the senior partner, and the elder of the two brothers. In those days it was always people with money whose sons and daughters were apprenticed to drapery and wholesale trades. The reason for this was, that a fee had to be paid, and among those who worked for a living, nobody only farmers could afford it. It was, as well as I can remember, usually eighty or one hundred pounds, riches to us, and far out of the reach of the families we grew up with, I think Kieran's second name was Liam, for although almost everybody called him Kieran, he would answer to this name in a surly manner. I went in to the shop one day on my way home from school. I think it was Kitty Quinn who was with me and we were both looking for a rope to use for skipping. The shopkeepers, in those days at any rate used to have rope tied around the boxes in which their goods would come. Kitty said 'have you got any rope Kieran', 'No I haven't' he replied in a surly manner. I don't know what made me ask also, after this reply, for in those days I had very little either moral, or physical courage. 'Would you have a rope for me Liam' I said, I have Máire he said, producing one from under the counter.

I am at the moment reading Canon Sheehan's, *Luke Delmege*, after an interval of over fifty years, and it brought back to me, two more people who were part of my childhood. They were Tommy Mahon and Nan Sheehan. Tommy Mahon was the nephew of my stepfather's son-in-law, Tom Furlong, and as Tommy's father was dead the Furlong's brought him from Wexford and reared him. Nan Sheean was the Furlong's maid of all work who came from, I think, it was Clonmanagh which is a village outside Kilkenny City. As I remember them, they were both in their teens. They spent every night during the winter, in our house until bedtime. One of their ways of putting in time on a winter's night was, to tie a length of twine to the knocker of a neighbour's door, go into the field opposite, and pull the twine. Of course when the occupant of the house came out there was nobody to be seen. I was always a silent companion on these exploits, for, when I was young, I wouldn't, as the saying goes 'say boo to a goose'. However, in due time Tommy entered Saint Kieran's College, to study for the priesthood. He was ordained for his own diocese, that is Ossory, and then was loaned for five years, to an Australian parish. Nan Sheean became a nun, in Australia. I know that they met at least once in Australia. Of course Nan never came back to Ireland again, for in those days nuns rarely came out of their Convents, they were virtual prisoners. Tommy did come back on a visit, but would not settle in Ireland again. He was seemingly given permission by the Bishop of Ossory to stay on the Australian Mission. In *Luke Delmege*, Luke comes back to Ireland, very reluctantly, for after his seven years in 'civilised company' in England he had nothing but contempt for what, at the time, he considered, his ignorant, backward countrymen and women. However, unlike Tommy he did not get permission to go back on the 'English Mission', so he had to try and get resigned to the fact that he would have to stay in Ireland. The priests in Ireland never lived at the same low level as their parishoners. They all had a housekeeper, and a man of all works. Maybe this was the reason that they always, or nearly always, condemned their people when they rose to fight for freedom, whether their fight was just or not. I would exclude Canon Sheehan, for he never, in any of his beautifully written books condemned those who fought to make this land our ours a better place to live in. In fact it was always just, for the people lived in awful poverty and even when whole families were turned out on the road, and their poor homes razed to the ground, the only home facing them, the awful Workhouse, the priests, in almost all cases, told them to be patient. Although I am an old woman now, I think I would rather die with a gun smoking in my hand, than live out my life in that awful place.

I remember when the 1921 Treaty was signed, and people thought it was a great victory, my mother didn't, she suspected the *wily* Lloyd George, and that the Irish Delegation would be tricked into signing an agreement which would not be to Ireland's advantage. She used to tell us that when Lloyd George was a child, his people were so poor that they had to divide an egg after it was boiled, and Lloyd George would get one half of it. I think she thought it was a great achievement for him, that he could rise to be Prime Minister of England when he came from such humble beginnings. She used to recite a doggeral for us, and unfortunately I have forgotten most of it, I say unfortunately, for it was very witty. I can remember the beginning, and the end of it. It began,

> Lloyd George no doubt
> When his life ebbs out,
> Will ride in a flaming chariot,

And it ended thus . . .

> And move a bit higher
> Away from the fire.
> And make room for that
> Lawyer from Wales.

Whoever wrote it believed that he was going to the nether regions, and not upwards to celestial bliss. On the day when the Free State Army moved into the Barracks, and the English Army moved out, we were let out from school early, to see the exchange taking place. It meant nothing to us children, only that we were free from school earlier than usual, but it is as clear in my memory as if it happened only yesterday, we children standing in the crowd outside the Barracks, and watching the exchange of soldiers.

My mother, when she was growing up, used to go on holidays with a friend who was a farmer's daughter, and lived a few miles outside the city. She used to tell us of a young boy who worked there, and who when he went to bed at night (and it was probably a heap of straw for his bed) used to be very sad that he was unable to stay awake long enough to enjoy the luxury of being able to rest. He used to be so exhausted that he would fall asleep immediately. I think, amid all the experiences that I have had during my life, the one thing I dread most is poverty. The awful fear that I would not have enough money to pay my bills at the end of the week, or month. The person who says money is not important is either a fool or a liar. Poverty takes all the joy out of life. I witnessed it with my mother. She would be so lethargic that the house would be neglected, and she would sit down most of the day, laden down with worry, and worry is the most energy sapping emotion there is.

We would have been far worse off only for the fact that my step-father was so good in the garden. He grew potatoes, cabbage, cauliflowers, radishes, celery, turnips, parsnips, tomatoes, parsley, all the vegetables that ordinary working class people used in those days. No matter what the weather was like, he never dug the first potatoes until the 29th of June, it was the Feast day of Saints Peter and Paul, and whether it had a religious significance for him, or not, I do not know. Another part of our poverty was, that we never had enough warm bedclothes, the winter coats which we wore during the day would be thrown over the bedclothes at night to keep us warm. I hated this because I always had a love of civilised living. In all the house we had one decent dressing table. It was beautiful alright, for it was made of lovely mahogany but it did not hold many clothes. We laid our clothes on top of each other on a chair. I would have loved any kind of a table of my own, especially during the month of May when I always made an altar in my bedroom in honour of the Blessed Mother. My makeshift table was an orange box, turned on end to make it high enough. On top of this I would put a cloth, and then a statue of the Blessed Mother, and two vases, filled, usually with primroses.

We also had May Devotions every evening at seven o'clock, straight forward devotions, without any trimmings, rosary and benediction, with the hymns during benediction sung in the glorious Latin. The last hymn , sung in English, would be in honour of Mary, the Blessed Mother. We never understood the meaning of the Latin hymns but we loved them. Last Sunday, which was the last Sunday of May, I thought I would go to the devotions, which were held in the Augustinian Abbey. I was terribly disappointed, but I must add that it wasn't the priest's fault, he said the set prayers, which were laid out for him, but it was firstly, the gloom of the Church, there were only a few lights on up near the altar, there was one boy to serve. The priest and server came out of the sacristy, followed by the woman who decorates the altar, she had a bell in her hand, and she came out into the body of the church, and during the blessing, which is given during Benediction she rang the bell. To me, there was nothing uplifting in the devotions, no glorious *O Salutaris*, or *Tantum Ergo*. We lost a lot when we ceased to use Latin in our church.

In those days we were not as clean in our persons as people are today. We had to draw every drop of water we used from an outside source, except when it rained, when we would have a barrelful of rainwater in the backyard. This, of course was outside, but was within easy reach, but one time we would always have to wash our feet was when we would be going to Holy Communion. My mother always insisted on this, and when we had them washed she would light a piece of brown paper and throw it into the basin of water before we threw the water out. Why she did this I do not know, and I never asked her, but I remember it was never newspaper but always brown. She had several maxims, one of which was 'God is nearer than the door'. Very often he wasn't, not in the sense my mother meant anyway. I have written that the only knowledge I had of my father's family is that they lived in Maudlin Street. I have now before me certificates from the Valuation Office which names several Loughmans (it is spelled Lukeman, as we pronounce it). There is a Patrick Lukeman, Walkin Street Upper, and a Lawrence Lukeman, and Martin Lukeman of Marnellsmeadows. These records go back as far as 1855. According to the late Dr. Mac Lysaght, the genealogist, there were Loughmans in Kilkenny as far back as the mid sixteen hundreds.

I visited Kilkenny about two years ago and I thought I would renew a friendship of my childhood. I could not remember my friend's married name, but I knew that she lived on the Dublin Road, in one of the row of houses which leads up to the building which, in my childhood days was the boys primary school, but is now the Parochial Hall. After a few enquiries I found the house where she lived, and my knock on the door was answered by a woman who exclaimed when she saw me, 'Oh my Godmother'. She was a sister of my friend Peggy, whom I was looking for, and I had 'stood for her when I was only eleven years old. In my young days, when we enquired who the godparents of a child were going to be, we always said 'Who is standing for the baby?', so I always said, I 'stood' for Mary Walsh. Although it must have been forty years since she last saw me, she recognised me from my likeness to my mother. It was her sister Peggy's house alright, and when I went in and met Peggy, we reminisced about old times but with a certain amount of sadness, for she and Mary were the only two left of a big family, and I and my brother Billy, who lived in John Street, were the only ones left of our family. The meeting brought back to me the time Neddy Walsh made his first confession. He was Peggy and Mary's brother. I cannot remember to whom he told the details of it, but it went as follows 'I stole a halfpenny on my mother, I bought a halfpenny worth of sweets in Winnie Keeffe's. I met my Eily' (his sister), and she said 'Where did you get the sweets', and I said, 'I got a halfpenny from Jamsey Callaghan'. Winnie Keeffe kept a small shop in Maudlin Street, and Jamsey Callaghan was the clerk of St. John's Parish Church. I am sure the priest smiled to himself, he knowing all those mentioned in the confession.

Thinking back on all this has brought back to me a rule of my mother's which we always had to observe after receiving Holy Communion. The minute we came inside the kitchen, before we would eat any food we would have to drink a cup or a glass of cold water. We were never told the reason for this, and maybe my mother did not know either, but probably her mother enforced this rule too. Thinking on it now as an adult, I think it was because it was the purest thing one could put into one's mouth after receiving Holy Communion. I don't think I mentioned yet that there was one child of my mother's second marriage, a boy, whose name was Michael. I think I must have been about twelve years old when he was born. I can remember clearly the day on which he was born. The midwife was in our house all day, and part of the night before, and he was not born until six o'clock in the evening. My mother used to say afterwards that she 'ploughed' the bed almost all that day, in agony. One did not send for a doctor unless one had three pounds to pay him, a fortune to working class people in those days. If eventually, there was no hope of the baby being born naturally, the doctor would then be sent for, and he would deliver the baby with forceps, but without an anaesthetic.

I was delighted at the thought of having a baby to wheel out in a pram, although the pram was a very old fashioned one, and a few times I saw people laughing at it, but I didn't care. I was so thrilled with the baby. I think it is worth mentioning here that in those days a woman didn't go out, even to Mass until she had been 'Churched'. It was a ceremony performed by a priest in the church, and until she had been churched she was supposed to be unclean. How giving birth to a baby, especially when each life was considered sacred and people with large families were lauded to the skies by members of the Catholic church, could make a woman unclean passes my comprehension. This practice has been done away with for many years, and it entered my mind to write about it only one day this week when my daughter-in-law asked me about it. I cannot remember how many years it is since this ritual ceased, maybe about twelve or fifteen years, and I wonder if all the women who have given birth to babies during these years are still considered unclean by the church to which I belong.

Seeing on television a few weeks ago, a programme on Arab Ponies, brought back to me a poem which my mother used to read to us from one of the volumes of *The Cabinet Of Irish Literature*. It was written by the Hon. Mrs. Caroline Norton. As children we loved it. It was entitled *The Arabs Farewell To His Steed*, and it went as follows.

My beautiful, my beautiful that standest meekly by.
With thy proudly arched and glossy neck, and dark and fiery eyes.
Fret not with the impatient hoof-snuff not the breezy wind.
The farthest that thou fliest now, so far am I behind.
The stranger hath thy bridle rein, thy master hath his gold,
Fleet limbed and beautiful, farewell — thou'rt sold,
My steed thou'rt sold.
Farewell — those free untired limbs full many a mile must roam.

To reach the chill and wintry clime that clouds the strangers home.
Some other hand, less kind, must now thy corn and lea prepare.
The silky mane I braided once, must be another's care.
The morning sun shall dawn again — but never more with thee.
Shall I gallop o'er the desert paths when we were wont to be.
Evening shall darken on the earth, and o'er the sandy plain.
Some other steed with slower pace, shall bear me home again.

Only in sleep shall I behold that dark eye glancing bright,
Only in sleep shall hear again that step so firm and light.
And when I raise my dreaming arms to check or cheer thy speed,
Then must I startling awake, to feel thou'rt sold my Arab steed.

Ah, rudely then, unseen by me, some cruel hand may chide.
Till foam wreaths lie, like created waves, along thy panting side,
And the rich blood that's in thee swells, in thy indignant pain,
Till careless eyes that on thee gaze may count each starting vein.

Will they ill use thee — if I thought — but no — it cannot be;
Thou art so swift, yet easy curbed, so gentle yet so free;
And yet if happily when thou're gone this lovely heart should yearn,
Can the hand that casts thee from it now, command thee to return.

Return — alas, my Arab steed, what will thy master do,
When thou that wast his all of joy, has vanished from his view.
When the dim distance greets thine eyes, and through the
       gathering tears,
Thy bright form for a moment, like the false mirage appears.

Slow and unmounted will I roam, with wearied foot alone,
Where, with fleet step, and joyous bound, thou oft hast borne
       me on;
And sitting down by the green well, I'll pause and sadly think,
Twas here he bowed his glossy neck when last I saw him Drink.

When last I saw him drink, away the fevered dream is o'er.
I could not live a day, and know that we should meet no more;
They tempted me my beautiful, for hunger's power is strong —
They tempted me my beautiful, but I have loved too long.

Who said that I had given thee up, who said that thou wert sold.
Tis false, tis false, my Arab steed, I fling them back their gold.
Thus — thus, I leap upon thy back, and scour the distant plains.
Away, who overtakes us now, shall claim thee for his pains.

We loved all the poems which our mother used to read to us, whether they would be considered great poetry or not I do not know, but they appealed to the sentimental side of our nature, and made sense. My mother had a poem of which I can remember just a few lines. It was as follows: 'What is all when all is told, this ceaseless striving for fame and gold'. There was a lot more in between, but it finished with the words, 'We are only here for a few short years, joyful or sorrowful nothing can last'. I don't think she was looking forward to the end of her life when she recited this, but we would be exceptionally short of money at the time, and the thought that it would end sometime used to console her. I know very little about my mother's family on her father's side, only that her father had one sister, whose name was Ellen. My mother and auntie used to call her 'the lady' on account of she being very quiet and gentle. She never married, but gave all her working life as a priest's housekeeper. The only memory I have of her is of going to see her in her old age in the home of The Little Sisters Of the Poor in Waterford. It was her wish to go there, for when she retired she went first to live in Kilmanahan (a small village about four miles from Clonmel) with auntie and her husband and small son. She was not happy there, for she was in the habit of going to Mass every morning and in bad weather she could not go even on Sundays. I think it was a priest who got her into the home, for it was not easy to get in there. I think all the old ladies there wore a long black skirt, a black blouse, a short black cape, and a black bonnet tied under the chin, almost identical to those worn by the ladies of the Salvation Army. To me, it didn't seem like an Institution, as they appear nowadays, for all the old ladies were walking about and chatting among themselves. My grandaunt was very happy there, and lived there to the end of her days.

In my childhood we never had dusty streets in the hot summer weather, for the corporation sent around what was called I think a watering cart. It was a square metal box drawn by a horse, with the driver sitting up in front. There were holes in the box through which a stream of water poured out on to the dusty roads. Looking at a man sweeping the road one day last week in a cloud of dust brought this back to my mind. When I started writing this I intended writing only about my childhood, the events of which are most vivid in my memory, but I think now that the amount I have written is not enough to have published in book form. I got depressed then, and thought it was all a waste of time, but some weeks ago a friend loaned me a book by Patrick MacGill entitled, *Children Of The Dead End*, an autobiography. He writes in chapter seventeen the following 'In this true story, as in real life, me and women crop up for a moment to do something, or say something, then go away and probably never reappear again. In my story there is no train of events or sequence of incidents leading up to a desired end'. When I started writing of my life, I knew not how I would end my story. When I started writing of my life, I intended writing only of my childhood, and unlike the writer of *Children Of The Dead End*, I thought I really knew when I would end it. I find now at this stage I haven't enough written to justify putting it into book form so although my life after my childhood is not so vivid in my memory, I will write of some of it as well as I can, and moreover, what I will write of, has not been written of in Ireland before now, but first I will write the words of another poem which my mother used to read to us when we were children. What especially recalled this poem to my mind is the fact, that, when I was in hospital in Dublin recently, there was another patient there to whom I was talking, and we both bemoaned the fact that children nowadays do not ever hear the poems which enriched our childhood, and she knew every word of the poem which I heard so often in my childhood.

CAOCH' THE PIPER
One winter's day, long, long ago, when I was a little fellow,
A piper wandered to our door, gray-headed, blind and yellow,
And oh how glad was my young heart, though earth and sky looked
    dreary,
To see the stranger and his dog, poor 'Pinch and Caoch O'Leary.

And when he stowed away his 'bag', cross-barred with green and
    blind yellow,
I thought and said 'In Ireland's ground, there's not so fine a fellow',
And Fineen Burke, and Shaun Magee, and Eily, Kate, and Mary,
Rushed in with panting haste to 'see', and 'welcome' Caoch
    O'Leary.

Oh! God be with those happy days, Oh! God be with my childhood
When I bareheaded roamed all day bird-nesting in the wild-wood,
I'll not forget those sunny hours, however years may vary,
I'll not forget my early friends nor honest Caoch O'Leary.

Poor Caoch and 'Pinch' slept well that night, and in the morning
    early,
He called me up to hear him play, 'The wind that shakes the barley',
And then he stroked my flaxen hair, and cried 'God mark my
    deary'
And how I wept when he said 'Farewell', and think of Caoch
    O'Leary.

42

Well twenty summers had gone past, and June's red sun was
     sinking,
When I, a man sat by my door, of twenty sad things thinking,
A little dog came up the way, his gait was slow and weary,
And at his tail a lame man limped, twas Pinch and Caoch O'Leary.

Old Caoch, but oh! how woebegone, his form is bowed and
     bending,
His fleshless hands are stiff and wan, aye — time is even blending
The colours on his threadbare bag, and 'Pinch' is twice as hairy,
And 'thin-spare' as when first I saw himself and Caoch O'Leary.

God's blessing here the wanderer cried, far, far, be hells black viper,
Does anybody hereabouts remember Caoch the piper.
With swelling heart I grasped his hand, the old man murmured
     dearie,
Are you the silky-headed child, that loved poor Caoch O'Leary.

Yes, yes, I said, the wanderer wept, as if his heart was breaking,
And where a 'vic machree' he sobbed, is all the merry making
I found here twenty years ago, my 'tale' I sighed might weary,
Son of my heart enough to say there's none but me, to
     welcome Caoch O'Leary.

Vo, vo, vo, the old man cried, and wrung his hands in sorrow.
Pray let me in astore machree, and I'll go home tomorrow,
My 'peace is made', I'll calmly leave, this world so cold and weary,
And you shall keep my pipes and dog, and pray for Caoch O'Leary.

With 'Pinch' I watched his bed that night, next day his wish was
     granted,
He died and Father James was brought, and the Requiem Mass
     was chanted,
The neighbours came, we dug his grave, near Eily, Kate and Mary,
And there he sleeps his last sweet sleep, God rest you, Caoch
     O'Leary.

Last year in the seventy fifth year of my life I realised a life long wish.
I visited Johnswell. It came about thus. One of my nieces and her
husband bought a house there, and she invited me over. It is about five
miles from the city, and I never knew until Berry, my niece told me that
it is part of St. John's Parish. It is a beautiful village, surrounded by
hills, but they do not close in on the village as might be expected but

43

enhance it. I was very eager to see the well the story of which had meant so much to me in my childhood. It adjoins the garden of my niece and her husband's home, and in fact they, and two other families in the village get their water supply from it. It is like all the other Holy Wells in Ireland, like a small chapel in structure, but attached to it is a concrete structure about sixteen feet long, and twelve feet wide, and about twelve inches in height. This I would think is where the Angel, Our Lady and St. John would come down at certain times, and as the description in the poem says would 'trouble' the water in the pool. There is no water flowing into the pool now. It is dusty and neglected looking, which is a pity. I also paid a visit last year to Talbot's Inch, as the walk out there in my childhood meant an awful lot to me. I went a way I had never gone before — up Green's Hill, and to this day I don't even know the name of the road which leads to it, for we always went to it along the Bishop's Meadows, by the banks of the Nore, and back home the same way. When we had driven about two miles the river came in view. There were a few people in swimming, and a few people leaning on the wall looking on. I asked a youngish looking woman were we near the Suspension Bridge. She answered that she had never heard of it, but a young man standing nearby told me it was washed away years ago in a flood.

This bridge was the second of the attractions as well as looking at the tennis players, which brought us so often in our rambles to Talbot's Inch. We would go backwards and forwards across the bridge, maybe twenty times enjoying the swaying of it. It was very naive of me to think that it would be the same after all those years. Later that year I paid a visit to Talbot's Inch and went out to it by the Freshford Road, which is the road which leads to the main entrance to the village. As children, we had never approached it from this road, and had never gone further than St. James's Park, which was then the G.A.A. grounds. I think it is now used as a Greyhound Track. The village looked completely different to me and I thought the houses looked different too, but they are not, for they were built shortly after the year 1906. Lady Desart bought the lands of Talbot's Inch in 1912. She had come there in 1906, March 17, and soon after built the village, primarily for employees working at the tobacco-growing or woodworker's industry. The houses are beautifully kept except for a few which did not look habitable, but men were working on them and they will probably be restored to their former state.

Chapter 5

With the Gentry in Kilsheelan and Leyrath

I said I could write of something which has not been written of in Ireland before now, that is, the life of a domestic servant. I have written earlier in this, the story of my childhood, of my mother's sister, to us children, our beloved auntie. She worked as a domestic servant all her life, or almost all her life, for, as I wrote in the beginning she had been trained as a dressmaker. She worked in Mount Bellow, in Galway, as a housemaid. I think the name of the family was Grattan Bellow. She then worked with the family of De La Poers. They lived in 'Gurteen La Poer', Kilsheelan, near Clonmel. I used to listen to auntie talking about the family, and listen with envy. Master Edmond, Miss Frances, Miss Valerie. The head of the family was Count De La Poer, his wife had the title of 'Lady'. It was a Papal title, Count of the Holy Roman Empire, and I realise now, it did not inspire amongst the 'gentry' the respect it would be given if it was bestowed by an English monarch, no matter how dissolute that monarch might be. One thing which auntie told us about life at the home of the De La Poer's, or rather the church where they went to Mass, which was Kilsheelan Parish Church, is that, one Sunday the priest said before he delivered his sermon 'would the people not go into pews which they had no right to be in (seemingly the better off people had their own pews) but would they go where they belonged, which was near the door'. I think if that happened now most people would never go into that church again. We do not think now that the priests are infallible, but I think that Catholics in those days did think that they were. I remember a priest in this parish giving a sermon on the Sunday before Ash Wednesday, and saying 'those who break the fast deserve to burn in hell for evermore!' I know he put the fear of God into me, but I would ignore it now. When I think of all the poor working class people, especially farm workers who did very heavy work, going out into the fields after a breakfast of dry bread and black tea, and

45

working until dinner-time, which was the only full meal allowed, with what was called a collation in the evening, which was six ounces of bread, and no more food until the next morning. Things have changed for the better now with only Ash Wednesday and Good Friday fast days instead of almost seven weeks of Lent. Indeed I think we have gone too far in the opposite direction now.

Auntie left De La Poer's after some years and came to us in Kilkenny for a while. My grandmother (my mother's mother) also lived with us at this time, but died when I was a little over two years old so I cannot remember her. I know from what my mother told me that she was of small build, very quiet and gentle, and that she smoked a clay pipe, and wore a black shawl when she went out. She was confined to bed for some time before she died, and I can remember as clearly as if it was yesterday what the doctor said to my mother when he called one day to visit my grandmother. 'My dear child' he said to my mother, 'If you don't get the patient off that feather mattress and on to a firm one, when she gets more helpless, you won't be able to move her'. It is strange the things that stay in one's memory. Probably it was the fact that he addressed my mother as 'my dear child'. I imagine he must have been a fairly old man. Where Auntie met the man she eventually married I do not know. I think it was at De La Poer's. He worked as a groom, and when they got married he was working for the Donoughmore family, at Knocklofty, outside Clonmel. After their marriage they lived in a cottage in the village of Kilmanahan, about two miles from Knocklofty. The cottage belonged to the Donoughmore family. Auntie's husband was Jack Foley, and his family were from that part of Tipperary. There was another cottage joined on to their's, and the people who lived in it were named Barry. He was a carpenter by trade, and I can remember well the distinction between a tradesman and a groom. I think the Barry's had a bit of land as well, which made them extra 'respectable'. I used to go there on holidays as a child, and loved being there.

I can remember Jack Foley served in the British Army for most of the 1914-1918 war, and I have an idea that was the reason the Donoughmore's employed him when the war was over. He helped to train some of the I.R.A. units during the War of Independence, but of course his employers did not know that. I can remember being on a holiday with them when the I.R.A. attacked the R.I.C. barracks, which was in the village of Kilmanahan. It was at night, and I can remember lying in bed, cowering under the bedclothes, terrified out of my wits.

Auntie had one child of her marriage, a boy. He was born in our house in Kilkenny, during the war. She was able to afford to pay a doctor because her husband was in the British Army, she would have had what was called in those days, 'separation money'. She must have been about forty years of age at this time, and terribly anxious to have a baby. Anyway, I remember my mother saying she had a long and difficult labour, and when the doctor came, and said he would have to use forceps, and would have to give her an anaesthetic, she would not take it, in case it would injure the baby. The baby was a boy, baptised William Anthony. When he was about ten years old his father got ill and in a very short time his illness was diagnosed as cancer. He did not live very long and a few days before he died Auntie wrote to my mother to ask if she would let me go and stay with her. My mother thought that if he was near the end I would not be of much use to her. This was a wise decision, for Jack died a day or two after my mother arriving. Where sickness and dying was concerned my mother had nerves of iron, which I have not, and never had. I don't know who made the decision, that Auntie should come and live with us in Kilkenny. All the contents of her little home were sold, and she and her son came to live with us in Kilkenny. That meant there were eight of us in the house, and no comfort for anybody.

By this time Paddy had left home for as soon as he had his apprenticeship finished, Stathams let him go, and as he could not get another job, he joined the Transport Corps of the Free State Army. I often think that Auntie would have been better if she had to stay in Kilmanahan, whether the Donoughmores would have let her stay in their cottage or not I do not know, maybe they would have wanted it for another of their workmen. Poor auntie never had a home of her own again, and when the money she had got for her household belongings was gone, she had to go out into service again. She went to work for the Bagwell family at Marlfield outside Clonmel. Billy stayed with us in Kilkenny. I didn't think anything of this at the time, but now, in my old age, with the memory of my own happy marriage, my three sons and three daughters, and all but one son near me, my grandchildren around me, and the stability of my own comfortable home, the pathos of it is almost more than I can bear. I try not to think of these things, and I do not like writing about them, but it is necessary to write of these sad events. Auntie didn't stay long working at Bagwells, and who could blame her, away from her child, and no relatives or friends near her. I don't think that my mother realised how awful this life was for auntie. She had never been away from her family, had never worked for anyone outside her own home, and didn't seem to have sympathy for anyone except herself. Maybe the poverty she experienced in her married life had made her hard, but she did not appear to realise the loneliness of Auntie's life. I have an idea that at this stage she looked for help from the British Legion, and the person who put it into her head to do so, was my Aunt Mary, she who embraced Michael Collins outside10

Downing Street. Auntie's husband had been wounded twice during the war, and my Aunt Mary told Auntie that she should look for a pension, on the grounds that his wounds could have been the indirect cause of the cancer which killed him.

Auntie did as she was advised and she contacted a Mrs. Price, who had something to do with The British Legion. Mrs. Price called to our house to see auntie. She didn't get the pension, but instead got an offer of work as a housemaid in Leyrath, an Estate situated about three miles outside the city. It was owned by Sir Otway Cuffe, and he and his wife lived there with, as their guest, or friend, the Mrs. Price whom I have already mentioned. The Cuffes had no children, and Sir Otway Cuffe inherited Leyrath, from an uncle. There was a belief among the people who lived near the estate, that the owners of it would never have a direct heir, also that there would be in local parlance, 'a hanger on', and in this case Mrs. Price would be that person.

Auntie accepted the offer of work at Leyrath and stayed there for several years. It is a large house with a beautiful entrance hall, a large stained glass window facing one at the top of the first flight of stairs, with another flight leading right and left, to a corridor, off which the bedrooms opened. There was one wing which was used as servant's bedrooms. These were in a very bad state, and in need of repair. Auntie and the other housemaid slept in one of these rooms. There was a curtain across one end of the room, it was about shoulder high, and behind this curtain was stored all kinds of rubbish. Old curtains and trunks, and I cannot remember what else. The only redeeming feature of this room, was that the window looked out on to part of the lovely garden. In the summer the house was always full of visitors, and I was employed there as an extra housemaid, at seven and sixpence weekly.

The staff consisted of a cook, kitchen-maid, parlour-maid, two housemaids, a dairy-maid, who considered herself a step above the ordinary domestic servants. She was a farmer's daughter, and would have received special training. There was also a coachman, for motor cars were few in those days, a steward, I should say I suppose a farm-steward, for he was over all the farm workers. I don't know how many of those there were, a fairly large number I would think, to warrant employing a steward. These two men, the steward and the coachman, both had bedrooms in the house and Mr. Burke the steward had his own sitting room. He didn't eat with the rest of the household staff, but had his meals served in his sitting room. He was always called Mr. Burke, while the coachman was always called Murphy by the family, and to this day I don't know what was his first name. Mr. Burke was an elderly man, and very nice mannered. He used to invite Peggy Newell, the other house-maid, and myself into his sitting-room for a chat. He

48

never invited auntie because like most elderly men he fancied young girls. Peggy was a very attractive girl, full of chat, while I was what Irish people would call a 'gom', which meant, that I had very little to say, and was painfully shy. The Cuffes did a lot of entertaining, especially during the Summer, when tennis was played on their own court. They always had the house full of guests for the Hunt Ball which involved a lot of extra work, as fires had to be lit in all the bedrooms, as well as the dining room and drawing room.

Domestic service in those days (I don't know what it is like now) was nothing short of slavery. 'Yes, my lady' to Lady Cuffe, 'Yes' or 'No' as the case might be, Sir Otway. But I must say that Sir Otway was one of nature's gentlemen, as distinct from being considered a gentleman because of his position. Lady Cuffe was every inch the 'Lady', haughty and distant in her manner. Mrs. Price was brisk and businesslike, but more approachable than Lady Cuffe. She was an Anglican Catholic, and never missed Sunday Service at Saint Canice's Cathedral. The women visitors were Madam, to married women, and Miss, so it would be Miss Rose, or Miss Elizabeth as the case might be. The visitors who stand out clearest in my memory are, Mrs. Tupper, and her young son. I think that Mrs. Tupper's husband was killed in the first world war. She was a quiet gentle woman, and always very caring where her child was concerned. I think her son must be the present owner of Leyrath for a friend of mine bought a dog from him some time ago, and she told me that Captain Tupper of Leyrath bred those dogs. It was considered more servile to call the young ladies Miss Rose, or whatever their first name might be, than just Miss, and no matter how young boys were, they were addressed as master. When I got older, I thought to myself if I ever get married and have children, I will do my best to give them a Secondary School Education, and I, and my late husband did just that. It is terribly demeaning that we Irish, descendants of a race of brave men and women, should be satisfied to live as virtual slaves in our own land.

The gentry of Ireland have always lived aloof from the real Irish, with a few exceptions. James Fintan Lalor described their attitude to Ireland very correctly when he wrote, 'Slaves to England and tyrants to Ireland, owning none and owned by none'. England has always been their spiritual home, not many of them take part in the social life of the community in which they live. At Leyrath, we, the staff were always very nervous, for we firmly believed that it was haunted, and one night, I, and Auntie, and Peggy Newell gave the whole night awake, for all night we heard footsteps going up and down the corridor outside the room in which the three of us slept. We were terrified and I went home next day and never worked there again.

I would like to recall one time in which Peggy Newell and I overcame our fear of the place being haunted, and on a November night when auntie was on holidays, (if one could call it a holiday staying in our home in the city for a few days) and when the dinner in Leyrath was over we took off to walk into the city. Strictly speaking we should not have been out at all, but the parlour-maid was there and would have answered the bell if it had rung. We walked down the avenue in fear and trembling as we were afraid a ghost would appear out of the bushes at either side of the avenue. No ghost appeared, and we walked the three miles into the city, and lo and behold weren't we rewarded, for wasn't there a torchlight procession, headed by a band. The procession was to commemorate the anniversary of the execution of the Manchester Martyrs, Allen, Larkin and O'Brien. These three men were hanged in Manchester Gaol (it could have been a public execution but I am not sure of this) after a trial which most people believed was not a fair one.

The only other memory I have of a patriotic commemorative procession and ceremony is on one Sunday afternoon, (I suppose it must have been on an Easter Sunday, because it was a lovely bright warm day) I would say I was in my early teens at the time, and some of my friends called and said there was a procession coming along Wolfe Tone Street, and as Wolfe Tone Street is just around the corner from Michael Street, we all rushed down to the corner to see it. It was going to Saint Maul's cemetery which is on the right hand side of the road as one turned around the corner from Wolfe Tone Street.

I have already written that I thought the procession was to honour a man whom I thought was named McEvoy, but when I was going through some papers this morning, I came across a letter which was a reply to one I had written to the Town Clerk, of Kilkenny Corporation, asking for information regarding the name, or names of patriots who were buried in St. Maul's Cemetery. The Town Clerk very kindly went to great trouble to get me the information I was seeking. I will give his letter in full, as Kilkenny City is such an important city now, and to give credit to Mr. Murphy. The letter was as follows:

18th August 1972

Dear Mrs. Healy,

I regret delay in replying to your letter of 22nd June last but I was trying to get as much particulars as possible for you.

There is a man named Morrissey buried in St. Maul's Cemetery. He was not shot in Friary Street, but was apparently shot around the old Kilkenny Jail during an escape break. The two men who were shot in Friary Street were Captain Thomas Hennessy, and Michael Dermody N.C.O., in the year 1921.

I understand that there is a stone over the grave of Mr. Morrissey, and that is recognisable, in the Cemetery. I also understand that Mr. Morrissey has a brother-in-law, called McEvoy still living, on the Callan Road, and he may be in a position to give you more information about this matter.

Yours sincerely,
James Murphy

I should say here that the only person I recognised in the procession on that sunny Sunday afternoon, was a man named Mick Dermody, who worked in Delahunty's hardware shop in High Street, and its only now, all these years later, that I realise that the Michael who was shot in Friary Street was probably a relative of his. I can remember well the escape from the Jail, for my uncle Dick and his family lived beside it and although we did not often visit there we went over at that time. The hole through which they escaped was right beside the high wall of the Gaol and was about the size of the wheel of a motor car. Mick Dermody's mother was a distant relative of my mother, although there was no contact between our families, and I never met the woman, but the relationship stays in my memory because my mother said that when Mrs. Dermody's child was born she had not one stitch of baby clothes to put on it, and the midwife said to her 'did you think it would come dressed and all'. My mother said she was a very innocent naive woman. I hope that they, the men who were shot are still remembered, and commemorated in my native city.

Chapter 6

In Service in England

When I stopped working in Leyrath I cannot remember how old I was, nor how long I was at home without working, but I got it into my head that if I got a job in England I would never see a poor day. We could not afford to buy a daily paper, so to the best of my knowledge it was in the *Irish Times* in the library on John's Quay that I saw this advertisement for a parlourmaid in the 'Manor House' in Woodmansterne, a village in Surrey. I answered the advertisement, and was accepted for the job. There were Mr. and Mrs. Lloyd, the owners of the house, Mr. Lloyd's two adult daughters Sheila and Joan and his son Michael who was still at boarding school. Mrs. Lloyd was his second wife. She had been a nurse and had been one of two nurses who had nursed his first wife through a long illness. They had nursed her at home. It appeared Mr. Lloyd fell madly in love with her. Her name was Sheila, but all the family called her Biddy. I don't know how long after the death of his first wife he married her, but when I went there, Mrs. Lloyd had just given birth to their first child, a boy. I don't think they had any other children, and the boy appeared to be a frail delicate child, and he did not live very long. I saw the announcement of his death in one of our daily papers a couple of years after I left there. It was strange that they had a delicate child, as Mr. Lloyd was a tall robust looking man, and Mrs. was what, we in Ireland would call a hefty looking woman.

Mr. Lloyd owned a factory for making tins, and all their money was made during the first world war when the food, which was sent to the soldiers in the trenches, was packed in tins. He always struck me as not being what I would consider a gentleman. He always stressed the word 'Master' in regard to the new baby, which seemed incongruous, in regard to such a small scrap of humanity. The baby's name was Patrick, and Mrs. Lloyd always referred to him as baby. Mrs. Lloyd seemed to be a very unhappy woman, and had no hobby or pastime, apart from being fanatically particular about the cleanliness of the house. Although there was a large household staff, two housemaids, two parlour-maids, a cook and a kitchenmaid, herself, Sheila and Joan worked all day, cleaning as well. The appellation 'dirty Irish' could not be applied to her, for she was Irish, born and reared. Three of the servants were Irish Catholics. A Church of Ireland girl from Derry, attributed Mrs. Lloyd's unhappiness to the fact that she had been a Roman Catholic who had given up her Catholicism and married Mr. Lloyd in a Registry Office, and attended services in the Church of England.

The church in Woodmansterne adjoined the Manor House, and the Lloyd family did not have to leave their own grounds to enter it as there was a gate leading into the church grounds. I don't think I was ever in the church, for like all Roman Catholics of those days I thought I would be damned for ever more if I entered a Protestant church. The English girls were near home, and if Mrs. Lloyd's moods were more than they could put up with, they could give her notice that they were going to leave, but the Irish girls would put up with a lot more, as they were so far from home. At one time she employed two girls from Castlecomer, Co. Kilkenny. They had never worked in a 'big house' before. The name of one of them was Nelly, she was the elder of the two. I cannot remember the name of the other girl. Nelly was a stoutly built, sullen looking girl, but she was no fool. I think that Mrs. Lloyd was anxious to get rid of both of them, but apparently did not like to give them notice to leave. She used to criticise their work, and usually it would be to Nelly she would complain. Nelly would listen, in silence, but one day she gave back as good, or maybe better than what she got from Mrs. Lloyd. Mrs. Lloyd said to her, 'I'll tell Mr. Lloyd on you', and Nelly replied 'what do I care about Mr. Lloyd, he's only one man, and he didn't make the world'. Both Nelly and her sister left soon after this, whether they were let go or not I cannot remember. We all thought they were going back to Ireland, but they did not. It was pathetic, for they were what one would call 'Green Horns', and were not fit to be without somebody to be responsible for them in a strange country. One could understand Mrs. Lloyd being anxious to get rid of them for they had no idea of the work to be done in a 'big house'.

Mrs. Lloyd had every material thing she could wish for, a beautiful home, cars, with a chauffeur to drive her any place she wished to go, but she definitely was not happy. The chauffeur drove Mr. Lloyd to the local railway station every morning to get the train to London, where his business was. The station was only a few miles away, so Mrs. Lloyd and the girls had the car and chauffeur at their disposal for the remainder of the day, until Mr. Lloyd was collected around six o'clock in the evening, but Mrs. Lloyd did not appear to need any hobby, only housework. The food which the staff was given was very good, and the best which I had had up to that time. Lloyd's house was the first place where I had a bath, for in Leyrath there was only one bathroom, and that was for the family. To this day I cannot understand why the people who never worked needed baths, and those who worked hard, especially the kitchen maid, who had to keep a big black kitchen range stoked, clean out the soot fairly often, and keep the range blackleaded, had to wash in a basin. This was normal practice at the time as the same circumstances prevailed in the house I worked in before my marriage. The house had a basement, a ground floor, a first floor, and a third floor. The staff lived at two extremes, the servant's hall, where the staff had their sitting room and ate their meals, was in the basement, and the bedrooms were on the top floor, as was the bathroom. All the rooms were very comfortable. Mr. Lloyd kept a well stocked cellar in the basement, as they entertained a good deal, mostly business associates.

They were not what one would call 'County'. What fascinated me most about the contents of the cellar, where all the drink was stored, was the port. It had to be strained through folded muslin. The muslin was laid over a silver strainer about half the size of a half pint mug, and the wine was strained through this into a decanter. There would be a half pint of sediment left which I believed was the sign that the port was very old and valuable. I think that before I write any further about my life in England, I should say that when I arrived there my first overwhelming emotion was one of despairing homesickness. Despairing, because I knew I could not go back home for a year, when I would get two week's holidays. Years afterwards, when I read one of the late Ethne Carbery's poems, I thought she gave the best description of homesickness I had ever heard, and I quote, 'There's a hunger of the heart that plenty never filled'. I duly went for my annual holiday, and at that time, one of the housemaids had given notice, and was in the process of leaving, so Mrs. Lloyd asked me if I could get a friend of mine in Kilkenny to take the job. I asked Kathleen Geoghegan, (one of the family I have already mentioned, who lived in the end house of our row of houses) if she would take the job, and of course, she, not being working and like all of us in those days, living just above the bread line, willingly accepted. She came back with me after the holidays. I was delighted to have Kathleen with me. She was one of the girls who formed part of my childhood, and one of those with whom I shared the twopenny packet of Woodbines. Kathleen did not appear to suffer the same degree of homesickness that I suffered, and settled into the new life quite easily.

A few episodes occurred while I was in the middle of my second year in the house, which made all of us a bit nervous. First, there was a ring at the door bell one winter's night while the family were at dinner. Margery Carson, who was the other parlour-maid, and I were waiting in the hall off which the dining-room opened. We would wait there between courses, and when each course was finished a bell would be rung to serve the next course. Margery pulled back the heavy curtain which was drawn across the hall door at night, but there was nobody there. The same thing happened again some nights later. Mr. Lloyd went out around the grounds when the bell rang the second time, but he could not see anybody. It made us all very nervous for a while but then we forgot about it. Some time after this Sheila Lloyd got appendicitis, and was operated on in the house. Their money must have been unlimited, for I am sure it must have cost a small fortune to have an operation performed in their own home. After the operation, and when Sheila was fit to travel, Mrs. Lloyd took her away, I think it was to Bournemouth to convalesce. While they were away there was another unaccountable happening.

One evening Mr. Lloyd and Joan went out for dinner. All the indoor staff were down in the servant's hall and the nurse was upstairs with the baby. One of the staff went upstairs to her bedroom, which was at the top of the house. On the way up she smelled smoke, and discovered that a cupboard on the ground floor was on fire. This cupboard held billiard cues, and how the fire started was a mystery. The fire brigade was called, and I can remember them pounding up the stone steps from the basement dragging their hoses along with them. They got the fire under control very quickly. When Mr. Lloyd returned he was naturally very upset. That wasn't the worst of it, for a few nights later another fire broke out, this time in the billiard room, the billiard table was alight (I should say here that these happenings occurred in the summer-time, when the evenings were bright, and they happened about eight o'clock, when one would think that it would be difficult for an out-sider to gain access to the house). This fire too was discovered in time and did not spread past the billiard-room. The strange thing was that Mrs. Lloyd rang that night, and on the phone said that she smelled smoke. This may sound far fetched, but it is absolutely true. I think that Mr. Lloyd suspected one of the workmen who lived in one of the cottages on the estate, for he gave him notice of dismissal sometime afterwards. I think that all the indoor staff were nervous after this second fire.

Shortly after this happened my mother wrote saying that she did not feel well, and hadn't been well for some time, and would I give notice and come home. Our wages were paid monthly, and we had to give a month's notice. I did this and went home, to the usual shortage of money, and all the worry that went with it. Kathleen Geoghegan stayed on at Lloyds and eventually married an Englishman and they went to live in Australia. When my mother's health improved, I looked for work again, as usual through the columns of the *Irish Times*. I answered an advertisement for a parlour-maid from Mr. and Mrs. Percival Maxwell of Tallow in Co. Waterford. They arranged to interview me in Hearn's Hotel, Clonmel, to which I had to travel by bus from Kilkenny. I cannot remember if they paid my fare or not but I can clearly remember that they were both present at the interview. I think they had been married only a short time, and were both young. Mrs. Maxwell was very attractive looking, tall, slim and dark. The wages they offered were thirty pounds a year, but there was a big problem for them in making a decision on whether to engage me or not as I wore spectacles, I was told I would look nicer without them. It seems incredible now when one thinks of the amount of the wages offered, and the work involved, that the wearing of spectacles would be an obstacle to employing me. I was quite normal in every way, about five feet seven inches in height, straight and slim and dark haired. If I got a million pounds this minute I cannot remember if they prevaricated in engaging me, or if they gave me a straight answer, but I think my mother was not anxious for me to work for them, and I did not.

I ought to state here the duties of a parlour-maid. They were not menial as housework went. They involved setting the dining room table, bringing in the different courses from the kitchen, and serving the main meals, which were luncheon and dinner. This meant bringing round the individual dishes to each person, holding them at the left hand side of the person being served, and they helped themselves. The table was cleared after each meal, and glasses, silvery cutlery, and the tiny coffee cups and saucers washed. The dinner plates and vegetable dishes went to the kitchen to be washed by the kitchen or scullery maid, and if there was only a cook, she washed them. The breakfast dishes, which would contain what Irish people in general call a 'fry', rashers, sausages and eggs would be brought in, in silver dishes and laid on an electric hotplate. The family usually helped themselves at this meal, and also at afternoon tea. This meal was usually at four o'clock, and was partaken of in the drawing-room. It was served on a large silver tray, filled with fragile china cups and saucers, and of course, what I would call dainty eatables. Wafer thin sandwiches, muffins in a round silver muffin dish, which contained hot water in the bottom to keep the muffins hot, and there would be several other kinds of cakes as well.

The ritual of afternoon tea — outside perhaps of the Shelbourne has never really taken on in this country. It became a fashionable social event in the 1840's, and soon became not only a British institution, but a mainstay of British life. Poor young Rupert Brooke, out there fighting the Germans, was plagued with such nostalgia for these afternoon tea sessions in the old Vicarage of Grantchester, that it enabled him to write the immortal lines:

> Stands the town clock at ten to three
> And is there honey still for tea.

I don't remember honey ever being served at tea-time, but there was always homemade strawberry or raspberry jam.

Domestic service was always considered a menial job, and I am sure it is still considered the same. Apart from a charwoman's duties, (she was usually hired in the big houses to scrub the floors in the working parts of the house, which were the kitchen, scullery and larder), the work was not laborious. What made the life so difficult was the long working day, and the feeling that one had practically no life of one's own. From seven o'clock in the morning until about eleven o'clock at night, one had to be on call if any of the family rang the bell, and the 'day off', did not start until ten o'clock in the morning, which meant that the only time one could have what is popularly called a 'lie in', was on holidays, two weeks every year. At home, before I started working, the work was laborious, everybody had deal tables and chairs, which had to be scrubbed with Sunlight soap and a scrubbing brush. The cement floors also had to be scrubbed, but when the work was done one was free to go out. Domestic service was no better than slavery, in those days at any rate.

The author's family outside 38, Michael Street, Kilkenny in 1916. Katie Loughman holds one year old Billy, Jim (Bimmy) peers between his father, Jim Loughman and his mother. The author is beside her mother and the two boys are Paddy (9) and Jack (7).

Staff of Kilkenny Asylum 1910. Mary Healy's father is fourth from left in the back row. Note the measuring tape which marks him out as the tailor.

The author's stepfather is third from left in the back row.

John Street, Kilkenny.

Parliament Street, Kilkenny.

Patrick Street, Kilkenny.

Mr. La Sales Terriere, Master of the Tipperary Foxhounds, with hunters and hounds outside Kiltinan Castle.

'A sup of Congo' at Canon Patton's last 'Thrashing'.

A group of Fethard men. Back row L. to R: Matty Tynan, Bob Hally, Dan Mullins, Dick Allen, Tom Walsh, Jack Hally, Connie Fitzgerald. Front row L. to R: Mick Bough, Paddy Butler, Paddy Daniel, Jimmie Holly, Christy Allen, Jim Hally, Willie Slattery.

Chapter 7

Working at Grove House, Fethard

I cannot remember how long I was at home without working after I came from England, but in 1934 I answered an advertisement for a job as parlour-maid, with Captain and Mrs. Barton, of Grove, Fethard, Co. Tipperary. They answered my application and asked to interview me in my own home, to which I agreed. It may seem incomprehensible, that employers should be so particular in engaging a person in what was considered a menial position. When one thinks of it, however, it is understandable. Domestic servants handled the mail of the members of the family, they knew most of the details of their daily life, had access to things of value, silver, just as an example, especially cutlery, which, if one was dishonest it would be easy to steal. In general, one was part of the family, even it if was in a menial position. Captain and Mrs. Barton engaged me at a wage of I think thirty pounds yearly. It may have been twenty eight pounds, I am not quite sure, but it was eventually thirty pounds yearly.

I arrived in Fethard in July 1934. I was met at the railway station by Mikey Tobin. He was Colonel Cobden's groom, and Colonel Cobden was Mrs. Barton's brother. Mikey was driving the Colonel's car, and I was conveyed to Grove in that. The railway station at Fethard is no more. It has gone the way of very many small stations throughout the country, and to me it is very sad, especially when one thinks of the awful labour which went into the making of the railway lines. If the railway lines had only been kept open they would have provided lovely places for people to walk in comparative safety, away from the busy roads, but as my mother used to say 'much wants more' and some people whose lands adjoined the railway line fenced off part of the lines, and in one place the line has been demolished to within a few feet of the beautiful stone bridge which spans part of Jesuit's Walk. The stationmaster's house has been kept intact and is occupied, and the Goods Shed has been made into a Folk Museum. Great credit is due to Christy Mullins and his wife Margaret for this achievement. It is a wonderful place to visit, and it is only lately I discovered that at one time the trains went right through the goods shed. I heard this from Christy himself on my last visit there.

There was a cook and housemaid employed in Grove, and I was by far the youngest. I would not be twenty-two until September of that year. Mary Brady was the housemaid's name, and she was, I am sure, in her fifties. I think she must have been with the Barton family for about twenty years. I know that during the Civil War the Bartons were ordered by the IRA to leave Grove, and they emigrated to Scotland. Mary went with them, and maybe this was the reason that they thought the world of her. They were nice to all their staff, but it was very obvious that she was their favourite. Luckily the Republicans didn't burn Grove House, furniture and paintings and carpets were left intact. I think the Republican Army realised later, the fact, that burning the houses of the Ascendancy did not achieve anything.

I'll go back now to the other member of the indoor staff at Grove, the cook Bridget Power. She was from Kilmeaden in Co. Waterford. She was twenty years older than I was. I was very lonely there at first, but by degrees I got used to it. I don't know if domestic servants wear the same kind of uniform now as they did in the old days. The housemaid and parlour-maid wore cotton dresses and large white aprons in the morning, and a white cap which covered most of the head. The dresses were usually pale blue, or pale green. At lunchtime these were changed to a black dress with a detachable white collar, a small white apron with a small lace trimmed bib and the bib was held to the dress with two small pins. The cooks always wore a cotton dress, strictly speaking it may not have been cotton, it could be linen, but it would naturally be of a washable material, a large white apron but I do not remember any of them wearing a cap. (In some houses there would be two or three housemaids, but on average two parlour-maids, or a butler and footman.) The parlour-maid or footman always answered the door bell, and collected the mail in the morning after the postman had gone. He would come at around seven thirty, or a quarter to eight, and I often came down early and opened the hall-door, and went back to bed until eight o'clock. (If I could only sleep like that now.) Mikey Croke was the postman's name and he used to cycle on his rounds, for he was a Fethard man, and his other two brothers were shoemakers and ran a thriving business. Two of Mikey's daughters are still here in Fethard. He had three daughters, one of whom died in her early twenties. I suppose after Mikey Tobin and Captain Barton and Colonel Cobden, Mikey was the fourth man I spoke to in Fethard, and that is why he stays in my mind so vividly. The question then arose of what name to call me by, as there was another Mary on the staff. It was this Mary who proposed calling me Maura, and that is the name I am known by to my friends in this town where I have lived for the past fifty three years, a town which I love very much, and in which I have very many friends.

Bridget and Mary had bicycles and always cycled into Mass on Sundays. I, of course, had no bike, so on my first Sunday in Grove, Captain and Mrs. Barton drove me in when they were going to church. Colonel Cobden went to church only on Christmas Day. Grove House is about two and a half miles from Fethard, but there is one entrance leading to a long avenue which is less than half a mile from the town. Mrs. Barton pointed that out to me and said that as their Service was always longer than ours I could walk back that way as it was much shorter than the main avenue. There were several gates dividing the fields through which this avenue went, and they were always full of cattle, hence the gates, whereas the main avenue through which motorists drove had only one gate at the road entrance which was always open. When I came out from Mass and saw how near to the town this entrance was (for the other main entrance must be a mile further on). I was afraid I had made a mistake, and I knocked at the door of the Lodge House just inside the entrance gate. The door was opened by a very pleasant looking woman, I suppose she was in her thirties. She told me it was the right entrance, and chatted to me for a while. She was the first woman I spoke to outside Grove House, her name was Mrs. Ellen Morrissey, and we remained lifelong friends. She was always in good humour and great company. It is still a mystery to me how she could be, for the lodge consisted of a kitchen and two small bedrooms and in this house she gave birth to eleven children.

In those days all women gave birth at home. There was no running water inside or outside the house, and they may have had a shed at the back of the house with a dry lavatory. The water they brought from the local creamery, which was at least quarter of a mile away. All this was accepted as normal at the time, but how apparently good Christians like Captain and Mrs. Barton, could allow this condition to exist passes my comprehension. It would not have cost a fortune to build on even one large room. I know that people who were not of the Roman Catholic religion thought Catholics were made to have such large families, but human nature being what it is, and people practicing any form of birth control being threatened with eternal damnation during sermons, and especially during missions, what could poor innocent people do. Joe was Mrs. Morrissey's husband's name and he was the complete opposite to his wife in temperament. He was a slightly built low sized man of a choleric disposition. He would often be so late in leaving the house in the morning that he would run down the avenue which was over a mile long and often without his breakfast. Johnny Burke, who used to bring in the fuel for the house would tell Bridget the cook, and she would send him out tea and bread and butter, on the quiet. He was a comparatively young man when he died and I don't think he was strong which would account for his testy disposition. But to go back now to my means of transport into Mass, after the first Sunday Colonel Cobden very generously gave the household staff five pounds every Christmas and he gave the five pounds to me before the second Sunday I was there to buy a bicycle. Five pounds was a lot of money in those days, especially as my monthly pay was three pounds three and eight pence.

I must say here that the food in the three 'Big Houses' I worked in was very, very good, much better than the food any working class person would have at home. It was the sense of almost being in prison which was hardest to bear, and having to be available for all one's waking hours. I spent eight years in Grove, and on the whole they were happy years. In most of the 'Big Houses' early morning tea would have to be brought to the bedrooms of the members of the family. This would be a tray with a pot of tea, a jug of milk and a bowl of sugar, and needless to say a cup and saucer, never anything to eat. I cannot remember the exact time this tea was served, but I would think seven thirty or eight o'clock, and then breakfast would be served at nine o'clock. No member of the Grove household ever had early morning tea.

Captain and Mrs. Barton entertained a fair amount. One visitor who came every year was a General Kelly. He was a friend of Colonel Cobden's, and was, like Colonel Cobden a retired officer of the British Army. He usually stayed for a month, and he always brought a bottle of whiskey, as a present to Captain Barton, which he always helped to drink. This was commented on by the family and naturally so, but not in his presence of course, one doesn't usually use what one brings as a present. Captain Barton's sister, Miss Rose Barton, also came each summer. She lived in England and always stayed one month. The usual people who visited for meals were, Mr. and Mrs. Ponsonby of Kilcooley Abbey, their daughter, they had only one daughter, their sons, one of whom was called Chum, another George and the youngest Harry. I would say that Harry was about twelve years younger than the daughter Noreen, she was the second youngest. The De La Poers were another family who visited Grove. They were the only family who always had a chauffeur to drive them, and he would come into the kitchen for his tea. Most of the visitors were invited only for tea. Mrs. Delmege was also a regular visitor. She was formerly Miss Freida Keane, and the writer Molly Keane, was married to a cousin of Mrs. Delmege's. It was mostly during the war years that I remember her visiting, for her husband Major Delmege was serving with the British Forces abroad.

61

She was very often invited for dinner and she would walk the three miles from Fethard, even in the winter, for petrol was in very short supply, and was used only in dire necessity. I remember that she always wore flat-heeled walking shoes and carried her high heeled evening shoes with her, and changed into them when she arrived. She was a very beautiful woman, tall, slender and graceful. Why I mention her beauty especially is that for years she was pictured regularly on magazines in advertisements for Ponds Cream. Her husband, Major Delmege, is like the late Sir Otway Cuffe another of nature's gentlemen. For many years, until quite recently, he passed by the house where I live, with his inseparable companion, his dog, and if I was outside he would stop for a chat.

As regards the people who were asked to tea in Grove, Mrs. Barton segregated her visitors. On one afternoon the Ponsonby family the De La Poers, the Congreve's would come. I cannot remember if Mr. Congreve had a military title, but his wife was Lady Irene, and was a daughter of a deceased Marquis of Waterford. On another afternoon the visitors would be Canon and Mrs. Patton, he was the Church of Ireland clergyman, the two Miss O'Connell's, whose late father had been the local doctor, Captain and Mrs. Hughes, and the Jubilee Nurse, that is what the district nurses were called in those days. The next category of visitors (who were always asked on their own), were Canon and Mrs. Leslie. They always came for lunch and stayed for tea. The reason they were the only visitors was the fact that Mrs. Leslie was Mrs. Barton's very dear friend, and they would chat together for the whole afternoon.

Canon Leslie was the Rector of Clogheen, Co. Tipperary. The Leslies had two daughters, the younger daughter was a teacher at Alexandra College in Dublin. She was drowned when she was only thirty years old. The elder daughter was a poetess, and she wrote under the name Temple Lane, which, I believe is the name of a lane in Clonmel. She wrote the beautiful poem 'The Fairy Tree'.

> By moonrise round the thorn tree
> The little people play;
> And men and women passing,
> All turn their heads away;
> From break of dawn till moonrise
> Alone it stands on high,
> With twisted twigs for branches,
> Across the eastern sky.
> They tell you dead men hung there,
> Its black and bitter fruit,
> To guard the buried treasure
> Round which it twines its root;

They tell you Cromwell hung them,
But that could never be;
He'd be in dread, like others,
To touch the fairy tree.
But Katie Ryan saw there,
In some sweet dream she had,
The Blessed Son of Mary,
And all His face was sad;
She dreamt she heard Him saying:
'Why should they be afraid?'
Why should they be afraid?
When from a branch of thorn tree,
The crown I wore was made.

But if your hearts a child's heart,
And if your eyes are clean;
You'll never fear the thorn tree
That grows beyond Clogheen.

Other visitors who have just come to mind are, Captain Perry and his wife. They lived in Woodroofe, just outside Clonmel. Captain Perry was Captain Barton's agent. He bought and sold all the cattle for Grove. I would say he was Captain Barton's closest friend, and on his visits, he and Captain Barton would walk for miles around the estate, inspecting and assessing the quality of the cattle. Lady Blunden of Castle Blunden, Co. Kilkenny, and her two sons were regular visitors.

Captain Barton used to dread, or maybe that is too extreme a word to use, but he used to have to watch the two boys, for they used to tease his dog through the window of the basement where he was kept, and Captain Barton, like almost all of the aristocracy, idolised dogs. I remember one.time when his dog was sick and would not eat for a few days. He came to the kitchen door one night after he had finished dinner and announced joyfully that the dog was better, he had eaten chicken which to ordinary people in those days was a luxury, they would not dream of giving it to an animal. Working class people didn't care about dogs in the same way. Their way of life was too grim, and they had not the time or the food to pamper animals. I should say here that Captain Barton never came past the kitchen door, nor intruded on our privacy. With all the rooms in the very large house the staff had only the kitchen to sit in, on hard backed kitchen chairs, in front of a black stove which was closed-in, and used to heat the water. We did not have even the luxury of looking at a flame. Grove House was more than large enough to give us a comfortable sitting room or a servants' hall as the sitting room for servants was always called. There was a large dining room, a large drawing room, both of which were used every day, a small drawing-room, which was never used, and a library, furnished with several armchairs in which the family sat after dinner at night during the winter months. After dinner in the summer the family sat in what was called Captain Barton's office. He kept all papers relating to the estate there, and did all his business there as well but this would be in the morning. I think why they sat there in the summer was, that there was a beautiful view over the fields, and a view of the river which flowed through the estate. This office was at the end of one wing attached to the house, with another wing at the opposite side of the house. To the best of my knowledge both wings had three fine sized rooms, one of which would have made a comfortable sitting room for Bridget, Mary and myself, which would have been nice to relax in, in a comfortable armchair after a long day's work.

In case it would be of interest to ordinary working class people, I will write the menu for dinner, in Grove at any rate, which is the freshest in my memory. The first course would be soup, which was always home-made, this course was sometimes varied, and there would be grapefruit or melon instead. Then the main course, which would be similar to what most people would have. This would be followed by a savoury course, more often than not sardines on toast. Then a pudding or sweet course which most people call dessert, but which, strictly speaking is not. This might be trifle or a bread pudding or a souffle, which is a beautifully light dish, whose main ingredient is white of eggs. The table would then be cleared of cruets, and jugs, and glasses, except for liqueur glasses. The dessert course would then be served. The dessert plates would be ready on the sideboard. They were always flowery plates, on which was laid a small mat, and on top of this mat a finger-bowl, which was a small glass bowl half full of water, On this mat and plate was placed a knife and fork, which had cream bone handles, and the prongs and blade were solid silver, silver would not discolour the fruit, and the dessert course really meant fruit, raw fruit always, for instance, peaches, pears, grapes, plums, etc; and with this last course the liqueur drink was taken. Most of these fruits were grown in the gardens of the three 'Big Houses' in which I worked. In all of these houses in which the appropriate alcoholic drinks were served with each course, I never saw any person the worst for drink. When the dessert course was finished the fingers would be dipped in the water of the finger bowl, and wiped on the large white table napkin which was always used for breakfast, lunch and dinner. After the dessert course, coffee was served, to finish the meal. The cups in which coffee was served were very tiny, and never more than one cup was taken. This was sweetened with sugar-candy — irregular shaped pieces of what the dictionary defines as 'sugar clarified and crystallised'. The napkins used for tea would be no bigger than a woman's handkerchief, but always lace edged and embroidered. Table napkins, these were always called. It was not considered correct to say serviettes.

I don't think that Captain and Mrs. Barton ever missed Sunday Church service. The family were the sole occupants of the gallery in the church. The gallery is not used now, as it is not considered safe. I suppose one could describe this custom of ownership of pews or galleries as renting them, for it was always well off people who had their names engraved on them in small brass plates. I think the Barton family must have been the only family of their class in the neighbourhood, to have right of access to the balcony. There were a few other families in the neighbourhood who would have been equal in status to the Bartons. They were the occupants of Tullamaine Castle, the Cookes of Kiltinan Castle, whose lands adjoined Grove. Coolmore, whose occupants were the two Miss Murphy's. They were Roman Catholics as were the Carrolls of Rocklow. The Miss Murphy's never visited Grove and the Carrolls seldom did. The occupants of Kiltinan Castle was Mrs Grubb, of the well known Quaker family. Mrs Grubbs daughter, Mrs de Sales La Terriére and her son and daughter also lived there. Mrs Terriére had one son and one daughter. Her son was called Rory, after Rory O'Connor, who with Liam Mellows, Joe McKelvey, and Dick Barrett were executed on the feast of the Immaculate Conception, December 8th.

It was most unusual for members of the social class to which Mrs. La Terriére belonged to even take an interest in Irish patriots, much less name their children after them, but Mrs La Terriére was an unusual woman in other ways. All the entrances to the estate were left wide open, and the numerous ponies which she owned were allowed to be ridden bare-backed by any of the young people of the neighbourhood who wished to do so. I should also add that the same applied to Grove, the people of Fethard and its environs were also welcome to go through the fields, to swim in the river at New Bridge, and one could go down the Grove Road, through the entrance which opened off that, along the avenue and out through the gate which opened on to the Killusty Road. The beauty of this walk is that one was on the way home all the time for the Killusty Road led straight into Fethard. All this freedom of access to the estates was never abused.

Chapter 8

A young woman in an old town

I am sure the Barton Estate must have contained thousands of acres for, just outside Fethard for at least three miles, they owned all the land on both sides of the road. The land on the south side was all forest, and abounded with pheasants and woodcock and when the shooting season opened Captain Barton would hold shooting parties. The guests would arrive about ten o'clock in the morning (all male), and all the farm workers would be assembled outside the front door, and would move off after the visitors, down the avenue, across the Grove Road, and into the forest where the shooting would start. The farm workers would act as 'beaters' which would mean beating the bushes with long sticks, so that the birds would rise out of them and then the 'sportsmen' would shoot. I should say here that it was only the young farm-workers who would act as beaters, to the best of my memory, about six of them. They would be led by the 'keeper', who was the man responsible for rearing the birds, and patrolling the estate during all of his working hours. He always carried a rifle on his shoulder while at work. I would think it would be to shoot crows, which might prey on the game birds. The sportsmen would return to the house for lunch at one o'clock.

The shooting would continue until darkness began to fall, when visitors and family would return to the house for tea, which would be as I have already described. When the visitors left around six o'clock they would each be given what was described as a 'brace' of pheasants, which was a cock and a hen pheasant.

A very large amount of birds would be shot, some would be given as presents to friends, and a certain number hung in the larder. The larder had wire on the window instead of glass, so that the air could circulate around the birds. Bridget used to pluck and clean out all the birds, for unlike 'Upstairs, Downstairs', she had no 'Ruby' to do the menial work. She was the best worker I have ever known, for she made all the bread (with the exception of the small amount which was bought for tea-time sandwiches) also brown and white biscuits, cakes, scones, jams and marmalade. She had no sink in the kitchen in which to wash up, but she used to go out through a short hall to the scullery and carry out the plates, pots and pans. This scullery had the back door opening off it, but no window. It was probably bad planning, and want of thought which created this situation, and workers put up with a lot of hardshardship in those days which they would not put up with today. It may be of interest to people who do not know anything about the lives of people who do not have to live 'by the sweat of their brow'. They did not even have to turn back their bedclothes at night, for around eight o'clock in the evening two of the housemaids (in the case of Grove, Mary Brady and myself, as there was only one housemaid) took the bedspread off the bed, folded it, placed it on the end of the bed, and folded back the bedclothes, far enough for the occupant to get into bed. I have been told that this form of 'gracious living' exists now only in the homes of very rich people.

There were lodges at the entrance to the four avenues leading to the estate. Two of them were small buildings, but two were lovely two storey houses. They comprised a large kitchen and leading off it a scullery and larder. A lovely sitting room, light and airy, three bedrooms upstairs, and one small windowless room, which Phil Tobin, the father of Mikey, whom I have already mentioned, called the shaving room. The houses were demolished by the present occupant of Grove, which I think was a grave mistake. Servants were expected to be available to the family for all of their waking hours, but in Grove, after the death of Mrs. Barton, Captain Barton and Colonel Cobden never rang a bell after dinner, which was served at seven thirty, so we were free to go out for an hour or two after dinner was over. The three of us always made our way to Tobin's for a chat with Phil and Mrs. She was his second wife, as his first wife died when his children were quite young. There were no children of the second marriage. They were always glad to see us, as their house was fairly isolated, but quite near Grove House. Phil had three sons and two daughters from his first marriage, but the only one who lived at home with them was Mikey. He it was who met me at the railway station when I arrived in Fethard. To the best of my knowledge Phil was retired from working in Grove when I came there, but his wife was the char-woman there and of course Mikey also worked there, so they were entitled to live in the lodge. Phil's proud boast was that he was almost arrested one day in the town of Fethard during the War of Indpendence, in the mistaken belief that he was de Valera. In his general appearance he was like DeValera, tall and thin, and he wore a long black coat and a black soft hat. He was illiterate, through, I am sure no fault of his. One thing he said which was considered very funny in those days, I will relate here. Two of his

67

sisters went to America, and on the evening on which they went, a couple of neighbours went in that night for a chat, as was common in those days, for there was no radio or television, and it was the only entertainment people had. One of the neighbours said to Phil, 'Are your sisters gone Phil', 'They are', he answered, 'they went across the fields at six o'clock this morning, they are in America long ago'. This answer would not be funny any longer. I am sure it would be over one hundred years ago since those girls went to America.

The awful heartbreak of those words 'they went across the fields at six o'clock this morning', has always stayed in my mind, for it implied that they went without anybody to accompany them, and I always wondered did they realise that they would never see Ireland again. In an isolated case an emigrant would return, but they were very much the exception, and Phil's sisters never did return. Phil was not a very strong man and was often sick.

Mrs. Tobin was always in good humour, and on the days when she worked in Grove she would be singing as she was scrubbing the floor of the large kitchen and scullery, for they had wooden floors and the scrubbing of them was hard labour. (Why people think that masses are necessary for people who slave like this, to get them out of purgatory, beats me for they put their purgatory over them in this world.) She would have the correct air of the song she would be singing, but often the wrong words. Johnny Burke, who used to carry in the fuel for the kitchen stoves, and to whom Bridget would always give a cup of tea and a slice of bread (this would be about eleven in the morning) used to listen to her in amusement, but one day the words of the song were so incongruous that John had to run out of the kitchen in case Mrs. Tobin would hear him laughing. I remembered the words of the song for years. Johnny was a self-effacing young man. He was so shy that one day Bridget forgot to put milk on the table for his cup of tea, and he drank it black sooner than ask her for the milk.

The Tobins were the nearest neighbours to Grove House, but to be accurate the Hall brothers, Paddy and Mickey, were probably as near. They were elderly farmers, and were bachelors. They had a sister who was a nun in America, and although in those days nuns were seldom allowed out of their convents, whatever Order she belonged to seemed to be one of the exceptions. She came home on holidays, and the Hall brothers asked the three of us to a meal in the evening. They gave us a beautiful meal, there was everything on the table in the way of eatables. Although it was unthinkable, in those days at any rate for a farmer to marry anyone without a dowry, and I am sure they would not dream of marrying a domestic servant, it did not keep Paddy from having romantic notions, for one day Mary Brady was going into Fethard by the back road, (which is what we called the Killusty Road) on which the Halls lived. Paddy was driving the cows along the road into the yard to be milked and Mary stood in against the ditch to let them pass. Paddy made a grab at her saying 'come ere me darlin girl until I give you a gentle embracement', The gentle embracement resulted in Mary having to go to Dr. Stokes and have her ribs strapped. What Paddy's ungentle 'embracement' would be like is unthinkable.

The following anecdote, regarding the Hall's parents, was told to me by a person whose family knew the parents of the Halls. On the day after the parents of Paddy and Mickey Hall were married, Mrs. Hall donned a sack apron and was going out to help on the farm when her husband halted her with the following words, 'Stay woman, stay the threshold is your boundary.' In those days the Hall's nearest neighbours would have been theTierney family, who lived in the lodge of Grove Estate which was afterwards occupied by the Tobin family. The father of the Tierney family was what is called 'the whipper in', to the Tipperary Hunt, the master of whom was Mr. Richard Burke, who resided at Grove at that time. One of the sons of the Tierney family, Willie, worked in Grove and was talking of emigrating to America. When Willie mentioned this to Paddy Hall, Paddy replied, 'Go Willie Tierney, go and don't stay like Paddy Hall looking over the Park Wall'. Willie Tierney did go, and at the same time went Ger Whelan, whose people owned a farm quite near Grove Estate. How Willie Tierney felt when he landed in America I do not know, but I do know for certain how Ger Whelan felt. During his first six months there, he lay on his bed every night when he came back from work and sobbed his heart out with love and longing for Ireland, and I am sure he would have given up what was a more improved way of life, improved materially at any rate, for one look at what Paddy Hall called, 'The Park Wall.'

Recently I was asked by a young girl did I know the name of the Rector who preceded Canon Patton in Fethard. I was delighted to know that a young girl was interested in people, who in the past made this town what it is today. She is a member of The Legion of Mary, and a very intelligent girl, so I thought thanks be to God our traditional bigotry is fast disappearing. I made enquiries and found that Canon Patton's predecessor was the Reverend Basil de Bornville, who came to Fethard in the year 1891, and was here until 1904, when he was succeeded by the Reverend Canon Patton, who died in 1943. Canon Patton was succeeded by Canon Hazleton, who was here until 1965. Mrs. Hazleton took an active part in the local branch of the I.C.A., which is, as most people know, the 'Irish Countrywomens' Association'. To the best of my knowledge Canon Hazelton was of a retiring disposition, but he did know his fellow town's people and I think it was at his request that my eldest son, when he was in Secondary School used to go up to the Rectory and study with his two sons. It is a sad fact that there is no clergyman in the Rectory now. Their numbers have fallen to such an extent that it is no longer feasible to have a clergyman resident in the parish. The Rectory is now occupied by a Miss Ffolliott, and is called Glebe House.

Canon Patton gave employment to a large number of local men — sometimes up to fourteen. He also employed school boys during the school holidays. I have not the exact acreage of land which went with the Rectory, but, within an acre or two, it was twenty acres, so every inch of land must have been utilised. He was a very philantropic, kind, gentle man, and when he died he was mourned by Protestants and Catholics alike. Some young people growing up now hardly realise there are other religions beside Roman Catholicism. They will know there are people of other denominations in the six Northern Counties, but they will associate them with violence and bigotry. The boys and girls who get second level education will know, but there are very many who do not reach this level. People of all denominations have something to contribute to the life and culture of our country. And last, but not least our greatest patriots were not of the Catholic faith, and when Pearse named the four men who have stood out above all others in the history of our country, three of them were not Catholics. They were, Theobald Wolfe Tone, Thomas Davis, James Fintan Lalor, and John Mitchel. Only James Fintan Lalor was a Catholic. Pearse wrote, 'if one had to add a fifth to the four I have named, it would be Parnell', another not of the Catholic faith, though Parnell was a constitutionalist, and sat in the British House of Commons. One might ask why did Pearse name Parnell in almost the same breath as four men who believed that only by the use of arms would Irish freedom be achieved.

The following words spoken by Parnell will explain why: 'It is given to none of us to forecast the future, and just as it is impossible for us to say in what way or by what means the national question will be settled-in what way full justice may be done to Ireland — so it is impossible for us to say to what extent that justice should be done. We cannot ask under the British Constitution for less than the restitution of Grattan's Parliament, but no man has a right to fix a boundary to the march of a nation. No man has a right to say 'this far shalt thou go and no further; and we have never attempted to fix the ne plus ultra to the progress of Ireland's nationhood, and we never shall'. This is one of the reasons why I think it is sad that the Church of Ireland members are diminishing, another reason is that it will give dictatorial power to the Church of which I am a member. Even in the last week in the year 1987 pupils of the Secondary School were sent down to the church en masse to go to confession. Some pupils' confessions were heard at the altar rails, some in the confession boxes and some in the sacristy. This might be alright for small children who might be frightened of being closed in, in a confession box, but for boys and girls from twelve to seventeen years of age it is very undesirable. When I was a child, a certain day was allocated for confessions for the entire school, and I always went in fear and trembling. Everybody should be free to go when they like, and be able to choose the priest to whom they feel most at ease with, in that way they will make a better confession, and scrupulous people will be happier. I miss seeing a Church of Ireland clergyman in this town in which I have lived for so many years.

I will now return to Grove House, and as I know the people of this town are very interested in everything pertaining to the town and its environs, they will be interested in the origins of the Barton family. When I worked there I happened to come across a small book entitled, *Fethard and It's Abbey*, written by an Augustinian priest named Fr. Knowles. In it he stated that the Barton family came originally from Bordeaux. Under this section in the book a line was drawn, and at the side of the page was written, 'quite wrong'. This fascinated me and I was very interested in finding out the origins of the family. I am sure now if I had asked Captain Barton he would have been only too glad to tell me, but as I have already written, I was shy and unsure of myself when I was young and I would not have dreamed of asking him. I now know a paper found at Straffan purporting to be *Memoirs of the Barton Family* states that, 'The head of the family was Barton; of Barton Hall in Lancashire, near Manchester: the last of that line was Sir Gilbert Barton whose ancestors received the grant of their lands from William the Conqueror. Later on a Sir Robert Barton claimed descent from a younger branch of Sir Gilbert's family, of which branch, seven brothers, in the reign of Elizabeth accompanied the Earl of Essex to Ireland one of whom named Thomas obtained a grant of land in Co. Fermanagh. (On one occasion, a Mr. Barton of the Fermanagh branch, visited Grove with his son, and his son's wife. I know their call was not expected, but Captain Barton was very pleased to see them and they stayed for the day. This was the only time in my eight years in Grove, that a relative named Barton visited there.

The Grove Estate is believed by the Barton family to have been bought in the year 1744, or 1745, and subsequently added to. The following is an extract from a book named *The Family of Barton*. It relates to a member of the family named Thomas, and the following paragraph is preceded by sentences couched in legal terms, which would not be of interest to the ordinary reader. I was always under the impression that the Everard family were as the saying goes there from 'time immemorial'. From the book on the Barton family which I have been reading, it emerges that the first of the Everard family had the lands of Fethard Glynn conferred upon him:

'It is observed in The State of Europe, page 10, that in the County of Wurtenberg Duke Everard founded a great University, at Tubingen — a neat and rich town upon the Necker In Germany — and, having two sons and two nephews (brothers) attended King Henry II to Ireland, where the elder for his valiant services in a great battle fought in the County Tipperary had ye lands of Fethard, Glynn and others conferred upon him, which were enjoyed by his posterity till lately sold to Thomas Barton, merchant, of Bordeaux. The said Thomas Barton was born at Curraghmore in the County of Fermanagh, about eight miles from Enniskillen, and in the year 1725 being then about thirty years of age established himself in business in Bordeaux, which he conducted with considerable propriety. During the French Revolution the business was owned by a member of the family named Hugh Barton, but as an alien, he was at that time not allowed to hold property in France, and he arranged with Daniel Guestier to take it over and manage the business in Bordeaux, whilst he, (Hugh Barton) managed it in Great Britain, without any formal act of partnership existing. The difficulty of carrying on business in such disturbed times at such a distance and under such conditions were necessarily very great; nevertheless, with a perfect trust and confidence in each other these two remarkable men continued to carry on the business each in their own name and respective countries as though independent concerns, until on the 1st of August 1802 a regular and formal act of partnership was entered into for nine years, which was renewed in 1811 by a mere exchange of letters, and still further extended in the same manner until the 1st January 1830 when the eldest sons of these two old friends, Nathaniel Barton and Pierre Francois Guestier were admitted. (Daniel Guestier died 6th September 1847 aged 92 years.) Their sons in turn succeeded them, and the partners of the old firm at the present time are their grandsons, being the sixth generation of Barton and the fourth of Guestier.' (*The Family of Barton*).

Any person who looks at advertisements on television today in the year 1988, will see the one for Barton and Guestier. But to go back now to the Everard family, I know they were Roman Catholics, and apparently, they were able to hold on to all their properties. I have been told that in the mid sixteenth century one of their family was a Jesuit priest who lived in Cashel. I have always heard their family spoken of with admiration here in Fethard, and I think this must be because they were Catholics, for very little else seems to be known about them. It would appear also from what has been told to me that, like a great many families they had what we call a 'black sheep', who probably squandered his inheritance.

Documents relating to purchase of Everard estate

'Copy Deed of Conveyance to Mr. Barton of the Estate in the County of Tipperary from the several parties under the Deed — This Indenture, made the second day of January in the year of our Lord God 1752 and in the 25th year of the reign of our Sovereign, Lord George the Second by the Grace of God ect, ect.' — a lengthy document executed by William Barton, on behalf of Thomas Barton, and the other parties interested, setting forth several sums paid to each, amounting together to the sum of £30,500 being the amount of the purchase money for said Estate.

27th March 1751 — Copy injunction to put Mr. Barton in possession of the Estate of the late Sir Redmond Everard, purchased under the decree of the High Court of Chancery in Ireland.

'Twenty fourth year of Our reign': George the Second by the grace of God, of Great Britain, France and Ireland, King, Defender of the Faith, and so forth, to the Sheriff of County Tipperary Greeting. We command you under the penalty of one thousand pounds, that immediately after sight or receipt hereof, in pursuance of an order of Our Court of Chancery in Ireland, made in a cause there depending wherein Alderman Richard Dawson (here follows names of parties), bearing date 27th March, instant, you put establish and confirm or cause to be put established or confirmed Thomas Barton or his assigns in the actual and peaceable possession of the Lands and Tenements within the town and tenements of Fethard — here follows the description of all the lands, etc. included in the purchase. And that you preserve and defend the said Thomas Barton, his tenants and assigns in such actual quiet and peaceable possession of the Premises and every part and parcel thereof, from time to time, according to the purposes intent and meaning of the said order, and herein fail not. Witness Our Justices of Our said Kingdom of Ireland, at Dublin, the 27th day March, in the twenty fourth year of our reign.

By the Lord Chancellor
of Ireland
An Injunction
Sheriff of County Tipperary — Return Injunction of possession given to
William Barton, Esq. for Thomas Barton Esq:
By virtue of the within Writ to me directed, I did on the 11th and 12th
day of April 1751, deliver to the said named Thomas Barton, Esq. the
full and quiet peacable possession of all and singly the towns, land,
tenements, and premises within mentioned, and have preserved and
defended the said Thomas Barton, his tenants and assigns in such full
quiet and peaceable possession of the premises within mentioned from
time to time, as by the within writ I am directed.

Oliver Latham
Sheriff

What makes me believe that the Everard family were forced to part with
Grove is the fact that an injunction was served on them. The Everard
family also had a town house on The Square in Fethard, which some
assumed afterwards became the Military Barracks. In what year, and in
what circumstances they vacated it nobody seems to know, but the
Military were well established there when Cromwell entered Fethard. It
has now been proved beyond doubt that the Military Barracks was never
the home of the Everard Family. According to Mr. Richard Everard,
who now, with other descendants of the Fethard Everards, resides in
Holland it could not have been their home. Mr. Everard in reply to a
letter of mine written to him on 13th September 1988 states, 'Its style
indicates that it was built in the 2nd half of the 18th century when the
period of the Everard dominance in Fethard had ended.' The view of
some of the members of the newly formed Fethard Historical Society is
that it was built in the early part of this century. Nobody knows if it was
built as a Military Barracks, but the fact that it fronts the Main St., and
did not have a surrounding wall, which any barracks which I have seen
has tends to the view that it was not a barracks originally. The ornate
surround of the front door and window directly over it also supports
the view that the building was not built to house Military Forces.

The Barracks was burned during the Civil War but the beautiful Ionic
surround of the hall door was preserved, and was set into the high wall
which existed on the Square until the wall was knocked to build the
present Garda Barracks in the 1950s. It must have been set into
another lower wall for there was a stone seat there on which people
used to sit, and which local people called the 'armchair'. This

'armchair' was always used as an altar during the religious processions of May, and on the feast of Corpus Christi, it would always be decorated with flowers and a statue. This beautiful doorway is now at the entrance to the Sports Centre on the Rocklow Road. Our former curate, Fr. Cunningham, was instrumental in having the Sports Centre built in 1974 and to him great credit is due, every sports amenity is available to our young people, and I must give credit to the members of our local G.A.A. club who gave part of their grounds for this project.

I had lent to me recently a book entitled *Victorian Architect* by William Tinsley. In the second paragraph of the book it says, 'William Tinsley had building in his blood. His father, Thomas Tinsley was a builder. His grandfather Sylvester Tinsley was a builder. His great-grandfather, an elder, was a builder. His maternal grandfather, Joseph Brouph (or Brough) was a stonemason. The building instinct came as a double inheritance. All of these men lived in Clonmel on the banks of the River Suir. It was in Clonmel that William Tinsley was born, on February 7th 1804 and so it is recorded on his tombstone in Crown Hill Cemetery in Indianapolis in the American Middle West. The following will explain why Tinsley is relevant to the people and places I am writing about. First he describes his building of Adelaide Cottage at Irishtown Clonmel, he says 'for his growing family'. In the Spring of 1847 and again in 1848 Tinsley did some more work for Colonel Wray Pallister at Comeragh. The first assignment was to repair the water mill and make plans to enlarge the cottage.

Two months after the first summons to Pallisters, Tinsley was hired on another mill project, this time at Abbey Mills at Fethard, by Robert Harvey. The work at Fethard continued from August 1847 until late in November 1847, when Harvey died and the operation stopped. The mill was finished, but in what year I do not know, but by the older people of Fethard it was referred to as Harvey's Mill. Eventually it was owned by the Coffey family. It ceased functioning in either 1933 or 1934.

At one time another Mill must have stood on the same site for in the process of restoration a small piece of stone was found and inscribed on it is Aby Mills. It was built by Patrick O'Connell in 1791. Aby would be the usual way to spell Abbey before Dr. Johnson compiled his dictionary. It is fairly obvious that the site on which the present Mill is built was once the property of the Augustinian Order, for the ruins of the old Abbey church adjoin the Mill at one part, and in those days the Order would have been self supporting, and even I can remember them owning a fair amount of land and growing vegetables and fruit on it. They also had cows which supplied their own household and sold it to some of the townspeople. Very dear friends of mine, one of whom was instrumental in arranging what we always called a 'date', with the man who later became my husband always got their milk there. One day, one of the daughters went to collect the milk, the cows had not all been milked and she was told to come back after a while. She went into the Abbey to say a few prayers, while she was waiting one of the priests was there also and he came over to her and said 'did you come into the church without a hat to show off your hair'. She had very fair hair, and was very pretty. She nearly died with embarrassment for in those days people were terrified of the priests, and moreover, she was dying of T.B. at the time, and did not live much longer. She died in her early twenties.

I will go back now to my life in Grove, and I think I should have described earlier my Christmasses there. Mary, Bridget and I always went to the six a.m. Mass in the Abbey. We would walk in and back up the short avenue. I cannot remember what Captain Barton gave us as Christmas presents, but Colonel Cobden, as I have already stated, gave us five pounds. Miss Violet Cobden, the Colonel's sister, who lived in Marlfield, always came and stayed over the Christmas holiday, and the three members of the family had their main meal, their dinner, at midday instead of at night. This gave us a lovely free afternoon for they always went out for afternoon tea on Christmas Day, and they had a cold meal in the evening. I think it was to Ponsonbys they went for tea, but before they went they always called the three of us servants into the library at three o'clock to listen to the Christmas message of King George the Fifth of England. The very close friendship which existed between the Barton and Ponsonby family is explained by the following paragraph taken from the book, *The Family of Barton*: William Barton of Grove, left six sons and three daughters. Thomas (M.P. for Fethard) the eldest son married Mary Ponsonby, great grand daughter of William, first baron Ponsonby (who was afterwards created Viscount Dungannon) and of Sir William Barker of Kilcooley Abbey, County Tipperary'. We, the staff, always knew that a member of the Ponsonby family would inherit Grove, as Captain Barton had no children, and this explains why.

After Mrs. Barton died we were free to go out in the evening, but suddenly this stopped. Mary and Bridget were free to go, but as the parlour-maid it was my duty to draw the curtains in the downstairs rooms and in the Winter they would be drawn early. There was no problem then if we wanted to go out after dinner. In the brighter evenings Captain Barton would draw them across the library window. One evening he asked me to draw them at a certain time, which I did. After a couple of evenings he said come back in ten minutes — its too bright to draw them yet. This went on for nearly a week, every evening it would be come back in ten minutes or thereabouts. I was getting madder every evening, two middle-aged healthy men, and one of them would not get up and draw a pair of curtains across a window. I suddenly decided I had enough, so one morning when Captain Barton came down to breakfast I gave him a month's notice. It wasn't an easy thing to do, for nice jobs in domestic service were difficult to get. He just said 'oh, oh', and left it at that. After breakfast was over he called me and asked me why I was leaving. 'Well sir', I said (always sir) 'you keep on bringing me in every evening to draw the curtains, I cannot go out for a breath of fresh air, and moreover if I want to wash my hair I have to do it on my half day off'. (In those days there were no hair dryers, not hand ones at any rate, so it meant a couple of hours before one's hair would dry). 'Oh', he said with a great relief 'if that is all, of course we will draw the curtains, and I am sure you know we would hate to lose you', so I stayed on, and that was the only time in my eight years there, that there was any discord between us. Both Captain Barton and Colonel Cobden were perfect gentlemen in their behaviour to us. But, to paraphrase Kipling when he wrote, (East is East and West is West and never the twain shall meet). Anglo Irish are Anglo Irish and Irish people are Irish and never the twain shall meet.

In almost all cases Anglo-Irish have given allegiance to the English Crown. There have been a few deviations, the most notable being, in my opinion at any rate, Erskine Childers, who brought the consignment of arms for the Irish Volunteers into Howth Harbour on the Asgard in 1914. He would have been a cousin of Captain Barton on the maternal side. He was also the secretary to the Irish Delegation in the negotiations which resulted in the Treaty with England in 1921. I have also read somewhere that he pleaded all night with the Delegates not to sign. I do not know if this is true, but it appears likely that it could be so, as he took the Republican side after the Treaty. Ernie O'Malley in his book *The Singing Flame* has described him as being, kindly courteous, chivalrous, aesthetic-looking consumed by the fire of his spirit. He had at all times been willing and ready to help in any and every capacity. He knew the mentality of the British ruling class better than anybody amongst Republicans, and so British publicity had endeavoured in every possible way to portray him as a sinister figure. He was captured in Bob Barton's house in Annamoe, where he had spent many young years. And also according to Ernie O'Malley, Winston Churchill in a speech the day after the capture of Childers had said with satisfaction that 'the mischief — making murderous renegade Erskine Childers has been captured. No man has done more harm or shown more genuine malice, or endeavoured to bring a greater curse upon the common people of Ireland than this strange being'. When Churchill described him thus, one may be sure that he was a good Irishman. He was shot on the 24th November 1922, by order of the Free State Government.

Another member of the Barton family, Robert Barton was one of the signatories of the 1921 Treaty. I feel proud that I have worked for a family who could produce such a man as Erskine Childers. My late husband, and the members of his family are also proud of the fact that at one time they had a farm on part of the land which is now Grove Estate. The ruins of their home were visible until a few years ago, and they were just inside the wall of the estate, quite near the Mullin Bawn. None of the Healy family do not know when the land went on them, or under what circumstances, but it must be a good many years ago, for my husband's grand-mother worked as a dairymaid in Grove, and the family lived on The Green in Fethard at least one hundred and fifty years ago. In the year 1887, the whole of Grove Estate was either leased, or rented to Mr. Richard Burke. Mr. Burke was apparently a very rich man, for he kept a large staff, both indoors and outdoors, and a pack of foxhouds which were famous far and near.

My mother used to say 'money talks', it is a rather obscure maxim, but I suppose it means that it can buy one almost anything. The following is one instance of what it can buy. The sacrament of Confirmation was being administered in the Parish Church in Fethard, and either a son or a daughter of Mr. and Mrs. Burke was one of those being confirmed. A prie-dieu was placed inside the altar-rails, and the member of the Burke family was confirmed there. The very nice young woman who told me this belongs to a family of what we call in Ireland 'substantial farmers' and had no 'chip on her shoulder' which a member of a deprived family might have. She also told me that at one time her family owned a pew in the church. The church pews had red carpets on the kneelers, and the name of the family on the side of the seat engraved on a small brass plate. There was also a door with a small lock on it and had padded cushions on the seats. This custom existed in almost all small towns in rural areas, and farmers and shop-keepers owned pews, but maybe it is not correct to say they were owned, but rather rented, and the priests were paid about twenty or thirty pounds yearly for them. In St. John's parish in Kilkenny, to which parish my family belonged, there were four priests all living in the one house. In the course of my search for information of things which happened before I came here (for to repeat a phrase which a certain gentleman in public life used a few years ago, I am a 'blow in') I was told the pews nearest to the altar in the church were reserved for the soldiers of the British Army. Mr. Burke and his family vacated Grove in the year 1918 and Captain and Mrs. Barton then moved in. All Mr. Burke's furniture, carpets and curtains were taken away, and Mrs. Barton's furnished the house completely, to her own taste. There is a custom in Fethard which is strictly adhered to, that no funeral ever goes through Barrack St., even though it is the most direct route to Calvary Cemetery, a detour is always made and it goes down Burke St., and up The Green. The reason being that Cromwell entered Fethard through Barrack Street. The following, I know, will be of interest to all Fethard people. I was often told that the town of Fethard was surrendered to Cromwell's Forces without any opposition. The following is from The Family of Barton, and proves that it was surrendered on negotiated terms.

According to the minutes of the old Corporation of Fethard, it appears that Thomas Barton, of Grove, was elected Sovereign of Fethard, Co. Tipperary, for the years 1788 and 1792, in succession to Lord Lismore. In 1799, Hugh Barton was Sovereign. In 1808, Thomas Barton was appointed Recorder of Fethard. In the years 1812-13-14 and 15, Thomas Barton was elected Sovereign. In the years 1816-18-19-21-23-25 and 29, William Barton was Sovereign. There are two remarkable documents carefully preserved by the Grove family; one the original *Articles of Surrender* drawn up between Oliver Cromwell and the Governors of the Garrison of Fethard; the other 'The humble petition of James Everard on behalf of the inhabitants of the town, to his Highness, the Lord Protector'. The following is a copy of the 'Surrender', so far as it is decipherable:

'Articles of Agreement made and concluded on the 3rd day of February, 1650, between the Most Honourable Oliver Cromwell, the Lord Lieutenant, Governor of Ireland, and Lieut. Col. Pierce Butler, Governor of the town of Fethard, concerning the surrender of said town, as follows, viz: Imprimis. — That all officers and soldiers shall march freely with their horses and arms, and all their goods and baggage, colours flying, matches lighted, ball in pouch, out into any place within His Majesty's quarters or garrison, except such as are now besieged, safely conveyed thither free from any violence from any of the Parliamentary Guards.

Second — That all the country families and inhabitants of the town, also any of the officers may freely enjoy their goods, in town or abroad; as if they, or any of them, feel disposed to betake themselves to their habitations in the country, that they may have respite of time for that, and admittance to enjoy their holdings within contribution as others enjoyed to carry with them safely such goods as they have with them in this garrison.

Third — That all the Clergymen and Chaplains to . . . both of the town and country, now in garrison, may freely march with bag and baggage, without hindrance in body or goods.

Fourth — That all and every of the inhabitants of the said town, with their wives, children, and servants, and all their goods and chattels, both within town and abroad, in the country, may be protected from time to time and at all times; and shall quietly and agreeably enjoy their estates, either real or personal, in as free and as good condition as any English or Irish holding his or their Estates in this Kingdom — they, and every one of them, subject to such contributions as the rest of the inhabitants of the County of Tipperary are subject to, in proportion to their estates and no more. In consideration of which the said Governor hereby engage himself that he will deliver up the said town with all things therein, except such things as before agreed upon, to be taken away with them by eight of the clock this morning.'

The inhabitants of Fethard when threatened some five years later with a confiscation of their estates, fell back upon their old compact, and pleaded that under its provisions they were to be secured in their lives, fortunes, and estates. 'We owe to your Highness', says the petitioners, addressing Cromwell, 'our immediate being, and are induced to believe that the hand of God, which raised you to supreme authority, and in your progress to it entrusted you to dispense His justice, hath moved you to secure us under the shelter of your precious anxiety.' At the foot of this petition of James Everard, there is the following 'written in its entirety by Cromwell himself:- Oliver P.

Our will and pleasure is that the articles granted by us to the inhabitants of the town of Fethard, be well and soundly observed, performed and kept in all things according to the sense, meaning and import of them.'

Whitehall, 7th August, 1655'

The officers and soldiers mentioned in the *Articles of Surrender*, would have been loyal to the memory of Charles 1, who was executed by beheading, in 1649.

Chapter 9

Married Life in the Town of Fethard

Fethard town when I arrived here had a population of approximately one thousand. The people of Fethard are very proud of the fact that it is one of the best preserved Medieval Walled towns in Ireland. I have also heard it said that its Square which is part of the Main Street is one of the largest, if not the largest Square in Ireland. Fethard was also the first town in Ireland to have electricity, which was generated from the river at a part which Fethard people call *The Kennels*. People thought that a pack of hounds must have been kept there at one time. I now discover that the word also means a *canal* or *channel*. Eventually the turbine was removed and installed in The Mill at The Valley, and this supplied the town with electricity, until the E.S.B. took over this task. When I came to Fethard this mill was owned by the Heffernan family who lived on The Green. It is now the property of Tipperary South Riding County Council. There is now no member of the Heffernan Family in Fethard, which is sad, for they were an old Fethard family but like many another they are scattered, and live in different countries. At that time in 1934, the Garda Barracks was situated in the Main Street. It was the residence of the Sergeant, who was Sergeant Campbell, and there were at least four Garda. I can remember clearly Garda Evans, Walsh, Cassells, and Fergus. Those of Garda rank had their own residences in the town, but they had their Duty Room in the barracks.

For some time after arriving here I was rather lost, for life in a rural area is very different from life in a city. One of the things which struck me most forcefully is the fact that people in rural areas are inclined to be more secretive in small things than people in urban areas. Some years ago I read a book, the title, and name of the writer I cannot remember, but a description of Irish peasants in it incensed me greatly. It ran thus, 'The ignorant secrecy of the Irish peasant'. My own belief is that in rural areas there was more insecurity, for most of the people were at the mercy of the Anglo Irish landlords, and, moreover, it was people in rural areas who mostly kept the spirit of patriotism alive, and if they broke the law one idle word (and it might be only in a small way) could land them in prison. I was very ignorant of everything to do with country life, for until I came to Grove every animal I saw in a field, which wasn't a horse or a sheep, was either a cow or a bull. I never knew there were such things as bullocks. After a while I got used to the different way of life, and to use an old-fashioned phrase I had a few 'sweethearts', at different times which helped to assuage my loneliness.

I had become friends with the Browne family of Burke Street. This friendship developed through Mary and Bridget who were close friends of the Browne's. They are all gone these many years. Anyway, I was pushing my bicycle up the steep hill outside the entrance to the main avenue of Grove Estate, on my way in to visit the Browne's, when this young man came alongside me, also pushing a bicycle. He was Ned Healy, and his family lived in the Lodge, just inside the entrance to the Estate. He asked me if I was the new girl in Grove. When we got to the top of the hill we both cycled into the town together. Just as we reached The Valley, a man came out of one of the houses and called Ned. He went over to him, and I went on my way. The man who called him was the late Paddy Fitzgerald, a carpenter by trade, as Ned was, and they were both working on the building of Our Lady's Hospital in Cashel. They were ready to cycle back there after the weekend at home. I was twenty-two years old at the time and I did not have any contact with Ned again for the next five years. In the meantime the Healy family moved in to live in Fethard. They rented the house named Inisfail, just opposite the Augustinian Church. During this time I had made other friends, the members of the McCarthy family of Burke Street. At that time there were the father and mother, their sons, Charlie and John, and their daughters, Teresa and Angela. Two other daughters, May and Margaret were in America. To this day Teresa is one of my closest friends, although she has been in America for well over thirty years. Lately she has come over on holidays almost every year and her brother John comes from England at the same time and they stay with me.

The McCarthys are a very old Fethard family and I have often heard Teresa speak of Dr. Charles McCarthy, a cousin of her fathers, who emigrated to Australia and of whom she seemed to be very proud. From this time on the friends I visited, always on my half day off and on Sundays, were the McCarthy family. Teresa used to alternate between moods of very high spirits and moods of depression, for Angela's time was limited. She was suffering from the awful disease of that time which also took my father. But when she would forget the fact of Angela's illness she would be very witty and often Angela would plead with her to stop for she would laugh so much that she would get a bad attack of coughing. It must have been sometime in the year 1939 that Teresa told me that Ned Healy asked Charlie if he would make a 'date' with me for him. Charlie had a barber's shop in Burke Street so into it we both went and Teresa said to Charlie: 'could you get Maura a nice young man'. 'I could', said Charlie, 'what kind of a man would she like'. 'A nice looking, fairly tall, silent man', said Teresa. 'Go on now', said Charlie, 'you've told Maura all about it'. The word silent as regards Ned was very apt, for he never used two words where one would do, whereas I am the complete opposite, and I never stop talking, but I suppose we complemented each other, for it did not stop us from having a happy marriage.

As usual I am going ahead too fast, for I better go back to the years of our courtship, three years in all but we should have been married, long before we were, if we had enough money. It was the year the second world war started that we began going out together. I was sending home as much as I could out of my small wage, for by then my stepfather was an old man on the old age pension which was very small. My mother, as she seemed to be for most of her married life (at least from the time my father had come out on pension), was always 'in want'. There was practically no building going on in Ireland during the war years, and Ned would get a job only now and again. In the end we decided we would get married secretly and that I would keep on working.

We got married on a Sunday morning at half past seven on the 29th of September 1942. Bridget was witness for me and Ned's uncle Mick for him. We thought there would not be anybody in the church, but one of the biggest gossips in the town was there. John Lucy was also there and he and Ann Donovan got married the year after we did. John was the antithesis of the gossipy woman, and would be a man of few words. The news was around the town in a short time. Ned Healy and Maura Loughman got married this morning and of course the usual speculation 'is it a have to' but it wasn't. I went back to work and Ned went home. I suppose it was a most unusual way to get married but all my life I seem to be fated to act in unconventional ways.

I told Captain Barton that I had got married (it was most unusual for married women to work in those days) he did not mind so long as I kept on working for him, which I did for just four months. In the meantime, Ned's uncle, Mick, gave us a small house which he owned on The Green. It consisted of a large kitchen and two small bedrooms with an attic, which was used by the former tenants. At the time we were given it Ned had a pony stabled in the kitchen, for he supplied his family with timber for fuel all during the war years, mostly bought from Mrs La Terriere from the Kiltinan Estate. Anyway, he removed the pony and started work on the house to try and make it habitable. In the meantime, I moved into his home in Inisfail where his mother and sister lived. The ceiling in the kitchen of our own house was nice and high, but the ceilings in the bedrooms were only the height of the top of the door, owing to the attic bedrooms being over them, one always had to duck one's head going into them. Ned raised the ceilings in the two rooms and did away with the attic, which was a great improvement, but the walls in all the rooms were in very bad condition. The ceiling in the kitchen, which was only canvas, swayed with the wind every time the door was opened. The roof was thatched and in a bad condition. He covered it with corrugated iron which at least made it water-proof.

The kitchen of my home in Kilkenny was dark, as the window was long and narrow, and after sufficient heat, light to me is one of the most important things in life. I think it was the gloom of the kitchen which has stayed in my mind. As I write now, I can see through the length of three fields, with cattle grazing in the fields, up to what was once The Rectory, and it is now named Glebe House, and from the back of the house, through three fields, up to the wood at the top of the fields, and all this from my kitchen windows. When we first moved in Ned's uncle bought us a turf range which cost £5.00. In this we burned turf (when we could get it for it was the war years) and timber. It gave out wonderful heat and the range lasted for about thirty years. For a long time we had only one bedroom for we could not afford to have the second bedroom renovated. My mother, when she came on a visit, was appalled at the condition of the house. While she was here Ned moved into his mother's house to sleep. I didn't mind the condition of the house, for at that time I was pregnant with my first child and was as happy as it is possible for any person to be in this world.

There are brief periods in every person's life when they are very happy, and this period was one of mine. At that time nobody went into hospital to have their babies, so my mother proposed that I go over to Kilkenny for my confinement, which I did. My baby was delivered after a long difficult labour, by a doctor, and attended by the same midwife who helped to bring me into the world. She was a Mrs. Sixsmith, and she lived at the end of Michael Street. The baby was a boy, and he was baptised in St. John's Church, the same Church as I was baptised in. He was christened Thomas David. Thomas after my husband's father and David after my stepfather, who had died earlier that year. Tommy, as we have always called him was born on the 10th November on Padraic Pearse's birthday, and as all my nationalist hopes and all my beliefs are due to my reading Pearse's writings. I was delighted that my first born would have the same birthday.

In May 1945, my second child, a girl was born, whom we had christened Catherine Mary, Catherine, after both her grandmothers and

Mary after our Blessed lady. For this confinement I had to go into St. Joseph's Hospital, Clonmel, for my late sister-in-law stated clearly that she or her mother would not have time to give any help. There was a very bad thunder and lighting storm all that evening but Uncle Mick, as we called him, drove me in and with me went a very good neighbour, Mrs. Finn of Burke Street. She died only last year, on the 6th July 1988, aged ninety-four years. Tommy was only one and a half years old at this time and Ned was a suffering from stomach ulcers, a complaint which was to plague him for many years. St. Joseph's Hospital was not then the lovely modern hospital it is today, but a bleak stone building. It had stone steps with iron railings and these were inside the building. The maternity ward was a long room with a timber floor which had to be scrubbed, and a small fire lighting at one end of the room. My great worry was, how will I tell Catherine when she grows up that she was born here. Now everybody in the area have their babies in St. Joseph's, except the women who like private hospitals, and usually they choose Aut Evan hospital in Kilkenny. My worry just goes to show how futile it is to worry about the future.

In May 1946, my third child, a girl was born, and was christened Ann Margaret. In the tenth week of this pregnancy I had to have an operation for the doctor who was present at the birth of my first child had been very careless and had done great damage to me during the delivery. I remember being brought out on a stretcher on a November night and looking up at the stars wondering would I ever see those stars again. I wasn't a bit afraid of death then, whereas now I am terrified at the thought. I knew afterwards that I had been very very ill, for when I was on the road to recovery one woman told me what she had said to another patient who was in the ward, 'I hope she doesn't die to-night anyway'. In the morning several doctors conferred around my bed, trying to decide would they or wouldn't they operate on me. A certain part of my anatomy had been badly torn during the delivery of my first baby and this part had now turned septic, with an abcess there as well. After great deliberation the doctors decided to operate on me the next morning. The operating Surgeon was Dr. Staunton from Freshford, Co. Kilkenny. He was there, I think in a temporary capacity, as the resident Surgeon was away. I was given an epidural, as it was thought a general anaesthetic might injure the baby. The operation lasted two hours and was a marvellous success, and to this day I have never forgotten the care and kindness I received from all the staff. There was a Sister Ignatius there, and to again use a hackneyed phrase, she was in truth a 'ministering angel' and it was she who looked after me almost all the time, except for the short time when she was off duty. I will never forget her kindness and care. I wasn't allowed any food whatever for ten days and one day when the dinners were being brought around I said to her 'Sister, when I am allowed food can I have two floury spuds and a lump of butter', 'Of course you can' she answered, and true to her word, on the tenth day, I got the two floury spuds, a lump of butter and a glass of milk. When I came home from hospital I felt so ill I used to have to sit down to wash the nappies. They were still the hard times of my youth, and for a long time after that for work was very scarce owing to the war. Most tradesmen went to England to work, but we managed somehow, and Ned's Uncle Mick was very good to us.

In August 1947 my third child, a boy was born, and christened James Matthew, James after my father, and Matthew after Matt Talbot who would keep him from having a liking for the 'bottle', an addiction which I dread. My fifth child, a girl was born in June 1949. I did not want to go back to Cashel hospital again for the nurse who attended me at the birth of Jim was far from being a 'ministering angel' so I went back to my mother's home in Kilkenny for the confinement. This time I was attended by a friend of my childhood who was a nurse, not a very close friend for she was several years older than I. It was she who used to hit the ball half way down the Street when we played rounders as children. As was usual with my first three children I had a long and difficult labour and at twelve o'clock that night the nurse went home, saying that the baby would not be born before morning. She left my mother alone with me, and three other children in the house. At one a.m. my mother called Nan Keeffe from next door, and if ever there was a living saint Nan was one. Her holiness was never obvious in as much as she didn't go to Mass every morning, but if ever one was sick or in trouble Nan was there, and she used to give hours praying when the other members of the family were gone to bed. I had intended if the baby was a girl giving her the names of Elizabeth Mary, for when I say the Hail Mary I always try to concentrate on the second mystery of the rosary when Our Lady visits her cousin Elizabeth, for to me, the whole meaning of the rosary, is in the words with which Elizabeth greets Mary. However, Nan said a few prayers for me, that I wouldn't be too long in pain, and then she said 'call the baby Concepta Mary'. She hadn't been born at this time, but knowing Nan as well as we did, and knowing that she had one unusual spiritual experience which only Winfie knew about (which Winfie had told my mother, and my mother told me) anything she would say would not surprise us. The baby was born at eight o'clock in the morning with the nurse present and also a doctor and of course she was christened Concepta Mary. My sixth and last child, a boy was born in March 1951, and was christened Edmond Oliver. Edmond after his father and Oliver after Blessed Oliver Plunkett.

Six children I had in the space of seven years and four months. I never considered the rearing of my children a burden, even though I had no running water for several years, and had only an outside dry lavatory. The only thing that I dreaded was the labour involved in bringing the children into the world, and with each child this was long and difficult. I suppose that if it was now I was having children I would not have had so many nor have had them so near each other, but in those days Catholics believed implicitly what the Pope, the Bishops and the Priests said, that all forms of birth control was a mortal sin. I do think that a large family is a great blessing if one has not to worry where the next meal is going to come from. Scarcity of money was again a problem during almost all the early part of my married life. In time we got running water and a bathroom, but it was through hard labour on my husband's side. He hacked through earth and rock to bring the water to our house, through what was once a quarry and he brought it from the Cloneen Road which was far away from our house. By this time we had acquired more space, or rather Ned's Uncle Mick bought for us another house adjoining our house. It belonged to a Mrs. Watt who lived in England, and it comprised two large rooms, with an attic over one, and out of this room a stairs led to the attic which was used as a bedroom. Ned took away the stairs and closed up the whole opening and put a trap-door in the ceiling and we made this room the kitchen. This room was the only part of the house which was slated, for the room adjoining this was also thatched, and covered with corrugated iron. We did not renovate this for many years as our family was growing up and we were determined that they would all get second level education, which they did. Tommy's education did not cost us anything, as he won one of the two scholarships which were given by South Tipperary County Council.

When I got married hardly any woman went into pubs. I was no exception, but it was no hardship for me, for, even today, penance of one hour in a pub or an hour on a race-course would be the hardest penance I could get. I did go out every Monday night to visit a woman who had young children like I had. For a very good reason I will not elaborate on this friendship. When I got older, and my children were more or less grown up, I used to visit Mrs. Finn in Burke Street. Her daughter Sally with Aine Tierney, who also lived in Burke Street and whose mother's maiden name had been Heffernan (a member of the old Fethard family whom I have already mentioned), were daily visitors to my house, and they brought my children out for walks almost daily after their school hours were over.

At this time her family (Mrs. Finn's) were all living, and working in other countries. Her husband was dead and she lived alone. Mrs. Finn,

Kathleen Conway, Mrs, Stapleton and myself would play twenty five until about 10.30, when Mrs. Finn would make a pot of tea, and the four of us would partake of it, with Mrs. Finn's homemade brown bread. We would go home about eleven o'clock. This lasted for many years, and in the course of time, like most things in this world, died out, but I always remember with pleasure and nostalgia those happy and enjoyable nights. Mrs. Finn was called to the Lord last year 1988, at the great age of ninety-four years. I was never short of neighbours calling in those days. Mrs. Heffernan, whose family I have already mentioned, was a daily caller. She would come in (the door was always open in those days) sit just inside the door which led into the kitchen and we would chat and exchange views. Another caller was Mrs. McInerney, who lived in Barrack Street. She would come in, just like Mrs. Heffernan, and sit on the same chair just inside the door. The difference in their visits was that Mrs. Heffernan would go home after her visit but Mrs. McInerney would go down the fields which led from my home and she would collect 'kippens' to light the fire, there were no such things as firelighters in those days. There is no such word as kippens in the dictionary, but they were small pieces of branches which fell off trees, and when they were dry they would light a fire faster than any firelighters. It was more a pastime with her than anything else, although a useful one. Even today when I go through a field, I pick up every small bit of dry timber that I can carry.

Mrs. McInerney was descended from an old Fethard family. On the maternal side from a family, one of whose members was a prominent member of the Fenians. I have before me as a write a cutting from *The Nationalist* of December 1938, which contains the following:

Mr. Bowe joined the Fenian Brotherhood almost at its inception, one of its founders was a Fethard man, Mr. Ml. O'Doheny, B.L., a leader of the '48 Rising and author of 'The Felon's Track' and threw himself wholeheartedly into the movement, and so quickly did his ability, fearlessness and enthusiasm become recognised and appreciated that he was marked out by his superiors for special work, and took part in many of the daring episodes that characterised the career of that organisation. Captain O'Delahunty and Gen. Burke, two Fethard men, having returned from America to re-organise Co. Tipperary, took Mr. Bowe in their counsels, and he assisted them at the secretarial work, and also carried all the most important dispatches to the several centres for them.

Arrested early in '67 whilst carrying an important despatch from Mr. James Walshe, chairman, Cashel Board of Guardians,

Killenaule, by military who had just camped at Kilnockan Cross, he was brought before a local magistrate, Colonel Kellett, Clonacody (father of the late General Kellett) to be searched as it was then the law that the military could not search a civilian prisoner until a magistrate was present. Colonel Kellett, who knew him personally ordered his release at once without being searched. Mr. Bowe had the despatch secreted in a pocket in one of his leggings.

Mr. Bowe was an uncle of Mrs. McInerney, and one son and daughter of hers are still in Fethard. The only one of Mrs. Finn's family now living in Fethard is Sally, who is now, and has been for many year's past, Sally O'Brien.

During all this time things were difficult financially and when I was six month's pregnant with Edmond the stomach ulcers, which Ned had suffered from for many years, necessitated his hospitalisation and he was so debilitated that it took eleven weeks to build him up to make him strong enough to undergo an operation. He was five hours on the operating table, and while he was in hospital, I went there also to have my baby, and we both came home from the hospital on the same day. After this, and when Ned was completely well again, things began to look up financially for us. Ned got work as a carpenter with the County Council, and as this job was 'permanent and pensionable' we felt secure as far as having enough money to live on went. We were then able to make our home more comfortable. We made a sitting room of the second room which had originally been part of the home of the Watt family, and we built a hallway, bathroom and utility room, and installed storage heaters in two of the rooms. One in the sitting room, and another in the room which originally had been our kitchen, for although the house is beautifully cool in warm weather, it feels cold and damp in Winter. The walls are almost two fee thick. As regards Ned's work with the County Council it was not onerous work, such as is involved on a building site, but almost all maintenance and I was glad for him, after a lifetime of what one might call 'hard labour'. At this time the maintenance of the hospitals was in the care of the County Councils, and he worked in the Council buildings and Saint Joseph's Hospital, Clonmel. Eventually the care of the hospital was taken over by the South Eastern Health Board, and he worked there all the time.

Meanwhile, our children were going out into the world, the older ones at any rate. Tommy sat for the Leaving Certificate Examination at sixteen years of age, but for a long time it appeared as if it was not going to be of much use to him in getting work. After about one year he got temporary work as an untrained teacher in a village school, a few miles outside Fethard. The Principal Teacher was ill with tuberculosis, and Tommy taught there for six months. When he was finished there it was the same story over again, no work for him in Ireland. Eventually he answered an advertisement which appeared in one of the daily papers. It was for a teacher in a boarding school in Newton Abbot in Devon, and it stated trained, or untrained. By a coincidence the man who owned the school was a Tipperary man and he called to the house when he was on holidays to interview Tommy and he engaged him. Needless to say Tommy suffered all the pangs of homesickness when he had to leave Ireland, and of course I suffered with him, knowing what he was going through. He used to come home three times each year and during holiday time I used to be so heartbroken when he would be going back that I would almost wish he wouldn't come at all. He did a teacher's training course in Saint Luke's Training College in Exeter, got married, studied for a degree, and got an external degree in Modern and Medieval History and Economics. He is happily married, has two daughters, aged sixteen and thirteen, a lovely home and quite enough money to live on comfortably as his wife is also a Secondary school teacher. But he still resents the fact that he had to leave Ireland for living in a country which is not one's homeland is like living for ever in the home of a stranger. All my sons and daughters were lucky, in so far as they have secure jobs which is a lot to be thankful for, and what I am more than thankful for, is the fact that they are all, with one exception in Ireland. I have nine grandchildren, all living near me, with the exception of the two grand-daughters in England, and they will be here on holidays this year and they love Ireland.

Chapter 10

The March of Time

In the Summer time Ned and I had a favourite walk, which was a little used passage-way at the back of Grove House, which led to what was called the Deerpark. There was no deer in it in those days, but what is still there are the stones of an old church and headstones. Two of Ned's uncles on the Healy side are buried there, they were twins, and they died shortly after birth. I knew the graveyard was called Kilmaclugh and I remember seeing funerals going along the passage-way when I worked in Grove. Our favourite walk was through the deerpark and over a stile in the wall of Grove Estate. Outside of this wall there was a road which led from Tullow boreen to the Kiltinan road. This road has now been incorporated into the estate of Kiltinan Castle, with a sign erected saying "trespassers will be prosecuted," but in those days everybody was allowed to roam the grounds of Kiltinan estate, just like Grove. We would go down the field, cross over on the wooden bridge which spanned the Clashawley River, and always go and look into what was known locally as the "boiling pot". It was a well, which to the best of my knowledge (and my memory, after all these years is inclined to be misty) gave out the same kind of noise as a kettle of boiling water, hence the name "the boiling pot". There was red stone at the bottom of the well, but local tradition told how a Bishop was murdered by being thrown from a height above the well. His blood stained the stone and it was never washed away. Ned and I were the last people to use this bridge across the river, for one sunny Summer afternoon, on our usual walk, I stepped onto the bridge, and when Ned stepped on to it after me, the bridge collapsed, and landed us both into the water, just up to our knees. To the best of my knowledge it was never rebuilt. Killmaclugh to me, holds many happy memories, memories of sunlit days, memories of Ned, and the days of our courtship, and moments of regret that I did not listen to more of the stories he could relate of local history. Rev. Dean Lee, (whose title is now Monsignor) has written about it in his *A Short History of the Parish of Fethard and Killusty*, where he states that the rectory of Coolmundry (Killmaclugh) was held by the Knights Templar of Jerusalem until the suppression of that order in 1307. It seems to have passed to diocesan clergy then.

Killmaclugh means a lot to my eldest son too, for like almost all Irish people who have to emigrate the love of Ireland seems never to leave them and a few years ago when he was home on holidays with his two daughters he expressed a wish to visit it. We drove down the Killusty road and up Tullow boreen got over the stile, over which his father and I used to go so many years ago. It was Killmaclugh my son Tommy was interested in but, alas it was inaccessible, most of it surrounded by barbed wire and overgrown with bushes and weeds. We came away very disappointed and sad. However, last year (1988) I heard that the graveyard had been cleared. I heard this from Mr. John Slattery, Drumdeel, and in November of that year I had the privilege of going into it with my daughter, and some of my grand children, and taking part in the recitation of the Rosary for those whom Catholics refer to as "the poor souls." Those are the souls who are still in Purgatory. This November rosary is organised by the local branch of the Legion of Mary. The graveyard has been cleared again this year (1989) by the following local men, Messrs John Slattery, Tommy Butler, Jackie Alyward, and Paddy Butler. It was a very worthy task they have undertaken and great credit is due to them.

I now write of the years that preceeded my widowhood. My husband, apart from the stomach ailment from which he suffered for many years, when he was a young man had, as the saying goes, the 'strength of an ox'. A little over fifteen years ago he contracted the ailment of shingles. He was in terrible pain, especially as he had them on his face and head, and on one of his eyes. His G.P. at this time lived in Clonmel. He prescribed pain killers, which did nothing to ease the pain, so eventually he went to a woman who had the reputation of being able to cure shingles. She had a bucket of water in the kitchen, and she put her hand into it and sprinkled his head three times, saying as she did so, 'In the name of the Father, Son and Holy Ghost'. I am not what one would call a superstitious person, and neither was Ned, but the pain went, and that was the first time he was free of pain for many days, and the first night he was able to sleep. Whether the water which was sprinkled on him was Holy Water or not he did not know. A few days after this he had an appointment to see his doctor in Clonmel. He was convalescing rapidly and on the Monday of that week he went down to the river and caught four trout. He also went to the river fishing on Tuesday, the trout were not rising, so he did not catch any fish. The following day, Wednesday, he went into the doctor, and he gave him an injection. He appeared alright that night but in the morning when I awakened he was lying beside me on his back breathing heavily. This did not worry me too much until I brought in his breakfast, and when I called him, he just sat up in bed, took the tray from me and didn't utter a word. At eleven o'clock, I brought in a cup of tea and biscuits. He was still sleeping heavily, and by this time I was getting worried. He came out to the kitchen at one o'clock, sat down in a small armchair which we had there and fell asleep again. Our small grandson came in, and he ignored him. He was our first grandchild, and as the saying goes, 'the apple of our eye'. When I spoke to him his answers were out of context to what I had said to him.

The next day Friday, our two daughters, Catherine and Ann came down from Dublin for the weekend, and Catherine drove him into the doctor in Clonmel. Ned went into the doctor's consulting room on his own, and when he came out the doctor called Catherine in and said to her, 'I cannot make any sense out of what your father is saying, he appears to me as somebody who has lost the will to live', and he gave Catherine a prescription for tablets for him. That was on Friday evening, and by Monday he was not improved in any way, so as a great favour, I asked the doctor whom I attended if he would examine him, which he did. He came to the house to do so and his opinion was that he had had a stroke, apart from not being able to know who any of his family were, he was able to walk perfectly and use his hands. The tablets which the doctor in Clonmel prescribed were what we call 'pep pills', so he told me to put them in the fire, which I did, and he also sent him into hospital, where he spent three weeks. He recovered slowly, and after three months was able to go back to work, and knew who everybody was. It was only some years afterwards, when I saw on television the effect an injection can have on some people, that I realised all his trouble stemmed from the injection. He worked on for a couple of years, but eventually had to retire for, although physically he was perfect, his concentration was impaired. He had a few year's of happy retirement, when he could stay in bed until ten o'clock in the morning, go down the town for his daily paper, meet the friends of his generation who are still around and have a chat with them. I thank God that he had, after a life of toil, a few happy years of ease. On the sixteenth of January 1980, we had just finished our mid-day dinner, and he and I had as usual, chatted a little during it, with I doing most of the talking for I am an inveterate talker, and Ned was still, as Teresa described him, a 'silent man'. When the dinner was finished he got up from the table and sat over on a chair by the wall. I cleared the table and put the dishes into the sink to wash up. I had my back to Ned, and as I started to wash up I said something to him and he didn't answer. I turned around to look at him and he looked at me mutely, for he couldn't answer.

93

He had in one second suffered a very severe stroke. He was completely paralysed on his right side, and was completely speechless. It is a terrifying experience to look at a person who has suffered a stroke. All I could do to keep him from falling was to wedge him in with the kitchen table and a chair, while I ran to my daughter, who lived quite near us, for help. She went and phoned our doctor but he was out and could not be contacted. We then rang St. Joseph's Hospital Clonmel, and they sent out an ambulance immediately. This was not usual procedure, for even as short a time ago as eight years bureaucracy reigned supreme, and it was not allowable to send an ambulance without a doctor asking for it. However, the man in charge of the ambulance section knew from the tone of my voice that I was desperate, and he also knew it was not a bogus call, for he asked me if it was the Ned Healy who had worked in the hospital, and of course I said it was. The stroke, and his loss of speech was almost unbearable, but what was to follow was almost as bad.

Just one week after he had been admitted to hospital, my youngest daughter went down to our doctor to ask him what were the chances of her father recovering. He told her that in ninety per cent of strokes recovery was up to the patient, or at least partial recovery, and he added, 'you know they won't keep him in there', meaning the hospital. When my daughter told me this the only word I can use to describe the way I felt is, flabbergasted. He was completely helpless, and I had assumed they would probably keep him six weeks and give him physiotherapy and whether it was successful or not we would then bring him home. On the Saturday of that week when we went in to visit him one of the nurses said to me 'the doctor wants to see you Mrs. Healy'. I went down to his office with the nurse. The doctor stood in the middle of the room. I would say he had just finished his rounds for he had his coat and hat on and was ready to go home. I waited for him to speak first, which I don't usually do, for I know I talk too much. The first words he said were 'poor Ned, very sad', and in the same breath he said, 'you know we cannot keep him here'. I said 'Why'. 'Oh', he said, 'we have sick people coming in all the time and we need the beds'. I replied, 'is my husband not sick, and very sick'. 'Yes', he said, 'but we will move him to Saint Patricks'. 'You will not move him anywhere' I said.

That was all that was said on that day. In the meantime the doctor sent for me again, to go in and see him in his consulting room. He told me that Ned would have to be moved. Now at this stage I had heard that the mother of a Local Councillor, who was eighty years of age, had been kept in the hospital indefinitely. I said this to the doctor, and I also quoted Karl Marx, or maybe half quoted him, for I said, Karl Marx said

'Workers of the world unite, you have nothing to lose but your chains,' I also quoted the paragraph from the 1916 Proclamation, 'Cherishing all the children of the Nation equally'. I also quoted James Fintan Lalor when he told the people of Ireland that 'Somewhere, somehow, and by somebody a beginning must be made' and I said 'I am making it now, but in a different context'. Nothing concrete was decided at this meeting, and all this time we were visiting Ned twice daily, and of course he was oblivious of all this controversy. On a third occasion he sent for me again, and it was in the afternoon, after visiting hours. I was still adamant that he wasn't being moved from St. Josephs. This was on an afternoon visit. It was the same over again, they would have to move Ned. In the end he said to me 'Go down to the Clinic' (the Clinic is in the hospital ground), 'and ask to see Mr — and see what he will say'. At this time I was as the saying goes almost 'at the end of my tether', and I was ready to collapse. I was brought into the office, and I felt so bad that I asked him for a glass of water which he brought me. I told him that Doctor — had sent me down to him. He left the room, apparently to ring the doctor. Anyway when he came back he proceeded to extol the advantages of the County Home. I planked the glass with the remainder of the water in it down on his desk, and said, 'you are welcome to it', and went out. The doctor had told me to report back to him, but I went home with my mind in a state of turmoil. I can say with Saint Ignatius Loyola, 'all my life I have loved justice and hated inequity', and to me this was injustice, for my husband had made Social Welfare payments all his working life, and he was entitled to proper hospital care when he was ill. My daughter, when we were going into the hospital the next day said to me, 'If the doctor asks to speak to you today you are not going near him for if you get any more upsets, we will have you sick as well as daddy'. When I was leaving the hospital when visiting hours were over the Nurse again approached me and said 'Dr. wants to speak to you'. I answered her, 'I don't want to speak to him, I've just gone through as much as I can take' (at this stage I and the members of my family were prepared to picket the hospital). 'I will go instead' my daughter answered, and she went down the corridor with the nurse. The nurse came back in a few minutes and said to me, 'the doctor especially wants to see you Mrs. Healy'.

I then went with her, and my reception was very different from the first day he sent for me for there were two chairs placed in front of his desk and my daughter was seated in one of them, and he told me to sit down. He said he had great news for me that 'Dr --- had arranged for Ned to be admitted to the Regional Hospital in Cork, and they may be able to do something for him there'. This was a great relief to me, and was a big change from moving him to Saint Patricks. His manner on this occasion I can only describe as being obsequious. My opinion was then, and to this day is, that when I didn't return to the doctor from the Clinic, he rang my doctor to know how far would I go, and my doctor, who knows that I am a 'fighter', told him that I would go as far as was humanly possible. Anyway, Ned was kept there for five weeks, as there was a strike of ambulance drivers in Cork at the time, and then he was brought to Cork Regional Hospital. I went down in the ambulance with him, and returned in the ambulance that afternoon. All that it was humanly possible was done for him there, but to no avail. He was not able to utter one word from the day he got the stroke, to the day he died seven weeks later. I, and one or other members of my family went down to see him every day (and I always say I never want to travel the road to Cork again, it has too many sad memories for me). Almost two weeks after he was admitted to the hospital there, the doctor in charge of him rang our doctor to say they could not do anything more for him there, and what did we wish to do. We said we would bring him home.

My daughter and a friend of hers went to visit him that day and I stayed at home to get the bedroom ready, and to clear a space for the extra things which would be needed to look after an invalid. When they returned they had bad news, for he was in the intensive care unit, as a clot of blood had gone to his lung, and his condition was critical. I, and the other members of my family went down to see him that night and the only consolation we had was that he had all the care and attention that it was possible to give him. After a few days the clot travelled to his heart and he died at three o'clock in the morning on the 7th March 1980. I will not dwell on the awful loneliness of living alone. Meal times were the worst, eating alone when one is used to company accentuates the loneliness, but time really is the great healer, although to this day, over eight years after his death I cannot bear to look at a photograph of him. I had to put any photos of him which were in the house out of sight after his death.

I was on my own in the house for a year and a half. I used to be nervous at night, and always locked my bedroom door, which is not considered safe to do, but I felt safer that way. In June of the following year the firm for which my eldest daughter worked in Dublin closed, and she came home, which for me was a great blessing, as she now works not very far away, and I am never alone at night. I have a good life for a woman of my age for I have young people as well as women of my own generation as friends, and every Monday night for about the past fifteen or sixteen years, we have what I suppose one could call a card party, seven of us, in each other's houses and a nice meal included. We play poker, which, if one happens to say it to one outside our group makes them almost gasp in astonishment, for poker is almost always played for large amounts of money, but we pay five pence to start play, open for five pence, and if one has a good hand, they bet either ten pence or twenty pence. Nobody either wins or loses much, and we always have a very enjoyable evening. On Wednesday nights I play Bridge, and then I have the other great love of my life, books. I am at the moment rereading Dicken's *Little Dorrit* and I am reading it with as much enjoyment as I did very many years ago. As I have written before, love of reading is one of God's greatest gifts.

All the members of my family are gone now. Bimmy died when he was twenty, Michael when he was twenty eight, Jack died in England when he was in his early fifties, Paddy died in the year '81 and Billy in '85. Bimmy is buried in the old Saint John's graveyard on the Dublin Road, with my father and grandparents and great grand-parents. Paddy is buried in Limerick, where he lived for many years, and where his sons and daughters still reside. Billy is buried in Saint Kieran's Cemetery, in Kilkenny, where his wife, sons and daughters live. All lived and died in, to use a hackneyed phrase 'in the bosom of their families'. All except Jack, he went to England with his wife when he was comparatively young. They had no children, and apparently after a while they went their separate ways. Jack ceased to write home but one month after his death my mother heard of it, from whom I do not know. She managed to get his wife's address and she wrote to her. She replied to my mother's letter and enclosed a letter which she had received from the hospital where he died. It is as follows.

20 — 8 — 58

Dear Mrs. Loughman,

I thought perhaps you would like another letter from me. Your husband was admitted here from Nottingham General in a very ill condition on Monday afternoon having already been anointed by the priest. On Tuesday morning I managed to obtain your address from their notes and wrote straight away. He asked to see a priest again at four o'clock and passed away very peacefully at six p.m. He suffered no pain at all. He lies now in our Mortuary surrounded by flowers. He looks peaceful, happy and most handsome. His funeral is being arranged now, and before I seal this letter I hope to be able to say the date so that you can send flowers here. He will not go without flowers, we will see to that. If you wish to come to the funeral you may come and put up for the night if you wish to.

Yours sincerely,
M. J. Kenshaw,
Matron.

Funeral 11.45 a.m. Friday 22nd.

The kindness and humanity of that letter is beyond belief. Any of my family at that time had not the means of going over, and seeking to find out where he is buried. I think it was a hospital for people suffering from tuberculosis to which he was moved. Maybe before this year is out I will be able to go over and find out where he is buried. It was only lately when I was going through some old papers that I found the letter. It is a sobering thought that I am the only one of my family left, but if my early life was hard and poverty stricken, I now have comfort, just enough money to live on, without worrying where the next meal will come from, and heat in the cold weather, heat which to me is one of the most important things of my life.

God took my husband eight years ago. I often compare my lot with several couples whom I know, who have reared large families, and in a great many cases have not one of them near them in their old age. In most cases their children had to emigrate to get work, and I realise that God has been good to me.

In Nora Connolly O'Brien's book *Portrait Of A Rebel Father*, she writes, that on the night before his execution, when she and her mother visited him, he said to her mother, 'you know what this means Lily.' Her mother answered amidst her sobs, 'but your beautiful life James, your beautiful life,' and he replied 'hasn't it been a full life Lily, and isn't this a good end.' I can echo part of that and say, I have had a full life, but I hope the end is not just yet.

Tipperary's Hurling Men

(On September 6th 1925 at Croke Park Tipperary defeated Galway in the All Ireland Hurling Final.)

Oh listen to the deafening cheer
That fills the air afar and near
'Tis Victory's slogan ringing true
For grand Tipperary's Hurling Men.
O'er Ireland's best they hold the sway
For Connacht's beaten in the fray
No hosts on earth could safely stay,
Tipperary's fearless Hurling Men.

Chorus
Give three loud cheers my country-men
For gallant Tipperary now,
Whose sons have honoured once again
The name and fame of Knocknagow.

On famed Croke Park's historic field
Where stalwarts struggled fought and reeled,
The Galway hosts were forced to yield,
Before Tipperary's Hurling men.
What Power could stay the onward dash
Of men who swept with lightening flash,
Like torrent down a mountain crash
Tipperary's gallant Hurling men.

From silvery Suir to Shannon's Shore,
From Slievenamon to Galteemore
The praise is chanted o'er and o'er
Of Tipperary's Hurling men.
The news is swept across the sea
To fill the exile's heart with glee,
And make him long again to be with
Tipperary's Hurling men.

Around the fireside's cheery blaze
When work is o'er you'll hear them praise
The Darcy's, Lahy, Powers and Hayes
Tipperary's matchless hurling men.
O'Donnell, Duffy, Cahill, Ryan
Are names Tipperary's heart shrines
For fearlessly they toed the line,
With Tipperary's hurling men.

Of Kennedy's deeds you'll hear them tell
Before whom many a fortress fell,
And Hackett too, who fought full well
With Tipperary's Hurling men.
They'll sing of Dwyer's and Kenny's fame
And talk with pride of Mockler's name,
The heroes of a thrilling game
With Tipperary's Hurling men.

God bless those men of fighting mould,
Who donned the famous blue and gold
And fought like heroes did of old
Tipperary's champion Hurling men.
And Ireland's cause is ever true
When she has sons as brave and pure,
As these from Shannon's shore to Suir
Tipperary's fearless Hurling men.

T. J. KEATING
Brookhill, Fethard